America's
DUMBEST
CRIMINALS

America's DUMBEST CRIMINALS

CRIMINALS

BASED ON TRUE STORIES FROM LAW ENFORCEMENT
OFFICIALS ACROSS THE COUNTRY

DANIEL R. BUTLER
LELAND GREGORY
ALAN RAY

Illustrations by Mike Harris

RUTLEDGE HILL PRESS®

Nashville, Tennessee
A Thomas Nelson Company

Published by Rutledge Hill Press, a Thomas Nelson Company, P.O. Box 141000, Nashville, Tennessee 37214.

Library of Congress Cataloging-in-Publication Data

Butler, Daniel R., 1951–
    America's dumbest criminals : based on true stories from law enforcement officials across the country / Daniel R. Butler, Leland Gregory, Alan Ray.
        p.   cm.
    ISBN 1-55853-372-9
    1. Crime — United States — Case studies. 2. Criminals — United States — Case studies. 3. Crime — United States — Humor. I. Gregory, Leland. II. Ray, Alan. III. Title.
    HV6783.B87 1995
    364.1'092'273 — dc20   95-30052
    [B]   CIP

Printed in the United States of America

18 19 — 05   04

To
the men and women
whose portraits and photographs hang in the
lobby of every police station we visited—
officers who were killed in the line of duty.
Under all the portraits and photos,
the same quote was displayed:

"Greater love hath no man than this . . ."

Introduction

The plans were all in place. The phone calls had all been made, the faxes sent, the interviews arranged and confirmed. Now the crew was on location, ready to set up and videotape our hilarious yet revealing interviews with police officers who had encountered America's dumbest criminals.

Time was money. With every moment, hundreds of expense dollars were clicking away. And here was the assistant chief of police, the man who had welcomed us so cordially the day before, giving us the kind of stern look that goes with "You're under arrest."

"You need to speak to the chief," he said.

We were ushered into a large office. Before us was a huge desk, and behind that desk was a very big man. To us, he looked like more than just an "authority figure"— he *was* the authority.

The chief did not smile. In that office no one smiled. And no one spoke but the chief.

"Explain to me," he said, "what it is you boys want to do."

Something in his tone made me think of every lie I had ever told. I swallowed. Then I launched into a nervous, chattering "pitch" for the home video series and book project we were trying to produce.

I explained that we had come to collect stories from the officers in his department about dumb criminals they had known. I told of my phone conversations and faxes to his assistant chief. I talked a little about our plans for a book and for television pilots.

As I spoke, I noticed a small plaque on the bookcase behind the chief's chair: "Treat the media as you would any other watchdog. Feed it, water it, pat it on the head, but never turn your back on it."

I finished my explanation. No one smiled. The silence seemed to last, oh, five to ten years. Finally, the chief spoke:

"Son, you need to understand something. You see, I was the interrogator on the Ted Bundy case. I went through that whole trial with the media. Then Hollywood sent me scripts for their movies-of-the-week and they asked me to circle whatever I thought was inaccurate. I circled a bunch of stuff and they went ahead and shot it just the way it was. Plus, in the last six months I've had two abortion-clinic shootings and I've had the media climbing all over my back every minute of every day.

"So tell me again," he said, "why I should let your cameras in here."

I saw our whole project teetering on a toothpick. I swallowed hard, opened my mouth, and miraculously, words came out.

"Chief, I've got two sons, seven and fifteen years old, and they love to watch television shows like *COPS, Rescue 911*, and *America's Most Wanted*. They think those programs are accurate, that they show the way it is for cops and for criminals most of the time. They think the crime scene looks exciting, even glamorous.

"I don't think that's true. I think that even the term 'Most Wanted' glorifies the criminals—sort of like a rookie-of-the-year baseball card. And from the few interviews we've done already, I'm convinced there's not much glorious about crime.

"In fact, I'm convinced that you police officers spend 90 percent of your time dealing with idiots—or with people just like me who have been caught doing the dumbest thing they've ever done. That's what I want to show in our videos and in our book."

This time the silence seemed to last ten to twenty years—without parole.

No one smiled. No one spoke. Except, finally, the chief.

"Son," he said, his face relaxing into something like a smile, "if you'll show criminals for the coldhearted dumb-asses they are, and if you'll show our police force as being professional at all times . . . well, then, we'll help you any way we can."

Over the next six months, this scene was repeated over and over. The stories were not all funny ones. With each officer that we interviewed, we felt the weight each one carries daily—the weight of pain and sadness and even fear. But police work, like any other stressful profession, is full of moments when situations take a turn for the absurd and when laughter seems as appropriate as tears. The most rewarding moments of this entire project came when the officers' very serious faces broke into broad grins and we all laughed so hard that tears came to our eyes. We hope this book shares a little bit of that laughter.

We want to make it clear, however, that in laughing at "dumb criminals" we are not making fun of the mentally challenged. We use the term *dumb* in the same way that great American philosopher Forrest Gump used the word *stupid*: "Stupid is as stupid does, sir!" We say, "Dumb criminals are as dumb criminals do, sir!"

Dumb criminals, in other words, are criminals who *act* dumb—people who opt for selfishness, ignorance, greed, or just plain meanness instead of using the good sense

God gave them. We take great satisfaction in showing the real and often hilarious consequences of such dumb choices.

None of the dumb crimes depicted in this book are still under adjudication. None of the criminals or victims described in this book are identified by their real names. All the stories really happened, but many details have been changed to protect the privacy of the people involved. The cops named in these pages, on the other hand, are very real. Their names and their stories are repeated with permission—and with deep gratitude. We wish them all the best as they continue to cope with the seemingly endless stream of America's dumbest criminals.

America's

DUMBEST
CRIMINALS

WARNING:
THE CRIMES YOU ARE ABOUT TO READ ARE TRUE.
THE NAMES HAVE BEEN CHANGED ...
TO PROTECT THE IGNORANT.

Never Mind

When Detectives Ted McDonald and Adam Watson of the Brunswick (Georgia) Police Department answered this particular home burglary call, they expected a routine report—missing TVs and VCRs, an empty jewelry box, perhaps a hijacked coin collection. But they were in for a big surprise.

As the two detectives drove to the address the victim had given them over the phone, they came upon a nice house in a middle-class neighborhood not far from their own homes. It was about five-thirty in the afternoon, and the victim had obviously just gotten home from work.

"The man whose house had been robbed was very upset," Watson remembers.

They could see where his sliding glass door had been pried open. It looked like an open-and-shut case of house burglary, one of several the officers had been tracking. But this victim introduced a new wrinkle in the crime spree.

"When we asked him if any belongings were missing from his home, he replied very quickly and indignantly that, yes, somebody had stolen his stash of marijuana. I looked at my partner in disbelief. We couldn't believe our own ears, so we asked him again just to be sure.

"Could you repeat that, sir?"

The victim's eyes got bigger as the cold, hard realization hit him. He had just admitted to a police officer that he possessed an illegal drug. He stammered for a moment in search of an out. There was none.

"Are you admitting to possessing marijuana?" the detectives asked. The man appeared to be frozen in time. He couldn't take the words back, and he couldn't think of any more to say.

"Sir? Is that what you're telling us?"

"I . . . uh . . . well, no . . . not really," the man stammered.

"Well, then, what are you saying?"

"Well . . . nothing, uh . . . I . . . oh, never mind," the man said. "Just forget it."

The officers turned and left as the man quietly closed the door, no doubt to sink into a chair and utter some expletives.

"We just left," Watson says. "Without the dope, we really had no case against the man. But we had a good laugh on the guy. And believe it or not, we've had several calls like that one."

The World's Shortest Trial

Officer David Hunter, retired from the Knox County (Tennessee) Sheriff's Department, told us this story of what might be the shortest trial in the history of jurisprudence:

At his criminal arraignment, the defendant stood before the judge.

"You are charged with the theft of an automobile," the judge said. "How do you plead?"

He expected to hear a simple "guilty" or "not guilty." Instead, the defendant tried to explain his whole defense as succinctly as possible.

"Before we go any further, judge," the accused man blurted out, "let me explain why I stole the car."

The judge's decision was made in record time!

Look Out! He's Got a . . . What Is That?

Our research has shown not only that some criminals are dumb but also that some use fairly weird weapons. Some of the oddest weapons used: an index finger, an egg, a bowling ball, a wedge of cheese, an artificial leg, a twenty-one-pound turkey, a hot-fudge sundae, a banana, a frozen sausage, a lit cigarette, a one-and-a-half-pound Chihuahua, an insect, a snake, and a toilet seat.

We can just imagine a dumb criminal attempting an armed robbery with a wedge of Limburger.

"Give me your money, or I'll cut the cheese!"

Positive I.D.

Detective Chris Stewart of the Brunswick (Georgia) Police Department told one of our *America's Dumbest Criminals* field reporters about a robbery suspect he transported back to the scene of the crime for a positive identification:

"We had gotten a call informing us that a woman had had her purse stolen from a shopping complex," Stewart says. "A short time later, we saw a man who fit the description given to us by the victim. So we picked him up and took him back to the scene of the crime."

Stewart explained to the suspect that they were going to take him back to the scene and that when they arrived he was to exit the vehicle and face the victim for a positive I.D. The man in custody heard this when the detective radioed ahead to the officer with the victim. Stewart said he had a man in custody who fit her description of the robber and they would be arriving shortly.

When they arrived at the scene, the suspect did exactly

as he had been told. He stepped from the car and looked up at the victim. And before anyone could say anything, he blurted out, "Yeah, that's her . . . that's the woman I robbed."

He has been given a new photo I.D. for his cooperation . . . and this one included a prison number.

Riches to Rags 5

Officer Brian Hatfield of Brunswick, Georgia, tells a sad story with a comical twist. He stopped a disheveled man behind the wheel of a fairly nice van that had sustained quite a bit of body damage. The driver had been weaving and was obviously a bit inebriated.

When Hatfield ran a check on the individual, he found several traffic warrants outstanding. So he brought the guy in for booking. The criminal didn't even have a dime for his phone call, much less the hundred dollars for bail. He called an attorney collect and then told Hatfield his sad tale.

"I won the Ohio lottery in April. Three million dollars."

"You won the lottery five months ago and you don't have a dime for a phone call?" Hatfield asked.

"I got the first installment, which was ninety-four thousand dollars. I went to Atlantic City and lost thirty thousand. Then I bought the van for thirty thousand, but

I got drunk on some really good French wine and rolled the van."

According to Hatfield's calculations, the man had frittered away most of his first installment, but not all. "What did you do with the rest of the money?"

"Oh," he said, "I spent the other twenty-four thousand foolishly."

D.O.B.

Officer Glen Biggs of the Knoxville (Tennessee) Police Department had a close encounter of the dumb criminal kind when he was booking a suspect on a narcotics violation. A simple transcript of the interrogation tells it all:

Biggs: "What is your D.O.B.?"

Dumb Criminal: "What's a D.O.B., man?"

Biggs: "When's your birthday?"

Dumb Criminal: "May 5th."

Biggs: "What year?"

Dumb Criminal: "Every year, man."

The two customers headed back to their pickup, oblivious to the uniformed officers and the two marked police cruisers in the driveway.

24

Drive Around, Please

J. D. Roberts has a colorful past. He has served as a member of the army's elite Delta Force and as a narcotics agent for the Drug Enforcement Agency. He has even worked security for some of Hollywood's top action-adventure celebrities. He now uses his expertise and experience as an instructor at the Federal Law Enforcement Training Center in Brunswick, Georgia. When we asked him if he had ever run into any dumb criminals, one incident immediately came to his mind.

One night Roberts was involved in a raid on a drug house that was doing a brisk business in marijuana sales. He and the other agents were dressed in black "battle" fatigues with "Narcotics Agent" stenciled on them. Local uniformed officers in marked police cruisers also took part in the raid.

Roberts and his team easily entered the house and apprehended the suspect. Several hundred pounds of marijuana were confiscated without incident. Within minutes, the officers were collecting evidence and finishing up at the scene.

As Roberts started out the front door, he noticed a pickup truck parked behind one of the marked police cruisers in front of the house. Two long-haired individuals got out of the pickup and strolled past the police cruisers parked in the driveway, then walked up to Roberts and his partner.

"Hey man, he still selling pot?"

Roberts looked at his partner, then back at the guy. "Yeah, he is. Just go around and knock on the back door."

"Cool." The two men nodded and walked on.

Roberts watched in amazement as the two individuals sauntered around to the rear of the house. Roberts radioed the officers still inside the house that they had customers at the back door.

The uniformed officers inside quickly hid while one plainclothes detective answered the door. The new customers asked where the old owner was, and the officer explained that the owner had stepped out but that he could help them.

They requested a fifty-dollar bag of marijuana. The officer went to the next room, grabbed a handful from the four hundred pounds of pot they had just confiscated and stuffed it into a plastic bag. The two customers were ecstatic. They thanked the officer for his generosity.

Roberts and his partner were still in the driveway, still wearing the black battle fatigues with "Narcotics Agent" stenciled on their chests, when the two customers headed back to their pickup, oblivious to the uniformed officers and the two marked police cruisers in the driveway.

Finally, Roberts walked up to the two satisfied customers and arrested them. The agents reconfiscated the dope and impounded the pickup—just as another prospective customer pulled up.

Roberts decided this was too easy to ignore. "We moved the two cruisers and started putting the impounded vehicles in the back. We made about fourteen more sales and arrests that night. By the time we were through, the backyard was filled with cars. It was the darnedest impromptu sting I've ever seen."

The Considerate Criminal

Working the front desk at a police station on a Saturday night is one of the most harrowing and maddening jobs imaginable. An officer can easily get behind in his duties when the phone is constantly ringing, prisoners are going in and out of the jail, paperwork is piling up, traumatized victims and witnesses are being herded through the hallways, and the miscellaneous weird people are wandering in. Bob Ferguson, an Indiana cop now retired, was working the desk on just such a night.

"A guy comes in around two o'clock in the morning and says, 'I'm wanted for robbery in Illinois, and I wanted to turn myself in,'" Ferguson says. "It just so happened that the desk I was working was located in Indiana. It was a crazy night, and there were a lot more pressing problems at hand than this guy. We were booking a rather violent guy on narcotics, and I had drunk teenagers throwing up in the lobby. Not to mention a prostitution sting that was processing about three hookers and five johns every ten minutes."

In the confusion, the officer blurted out, "That's all well and good, but I'm kind of busy. Either go to Illinois or come back at six." And at six o'clock on the dot, the man came back and turned himself in.

Bob Ferguson told the man how much he appreciated his punctuality " . . . then I politely booked him."

Taken for a Ride

Let's take a minute and flash back to the good ol' seventies.

Working undercover narcotics back then was a little more informal than it is today. A "flower child" mentality still prevailed in certain segments of the drug scene. This allowed for spontaneous and often funny moments.

At Purdue University, three undercover narcotics agents had been assigned to look for possible links to the drug culture. While cruising near the campus late one summer afternoon, they came upon a bearded hitchhiker with sun-bleached, shoulder-length hair. Peace signs adorned his Levi jacket and his army surplus backpack. Not having anything really pressing at the moment, the officers pulled over their Volkswagen van and offered the man a lift.

"Far out, man," he said, climbing in.

Soon the three of them were chatting with their new passenger as he babbled on about Nixon, Vietnam, and how much fun it would be to get high. Before long he had pulled out a fat marijuana cigarette.

"If you guys want to score really big," he offered, "I know just the place."

This was too easy. The agents eagerly agreed to take the man wherever he wanted to go. He'd make the buy, and they'd make the bust.

No one was home at the first house they tried. Their luck didn't get any better until the passenger remembered a dealer in another town. Would they drive the extra fifty miles to get the drugs?

"Sure, why not?" they said. After all, they were just out looking for a good time. Then, on a lark, they decided to pick up a friend of theirs, the crime analyst for their narcotics unit.

Now Roger, the analyst, didn't fit in with the rest of the group, who were all clad in leather jackets and sporting long hair and beards. Roger was clean-shaven, with a short, military-style haircut, and wore a tie and glasses. The passenger didn't seem to notice. He continued his friendly banter as he gave directions.

Before long the merry band of five was on its way in search of drugs, which the hitchhiker was readily able to supply. Finally, after a day of wandering from house to house, increasing their illegal stash at each stop, it was time for all good things to come to an end. Telling their newfound friend that they had some place they wanted to take him, the agents decided to wrap up the evening and drove him to the police station.

"This will be your new home for a while," the agents said to the passenger, who by this time was somewhat stoned and obviously flabbergasted. All he could do was shake his head as they explained they were police officers and that he was under arrest.

DUMB CRIMINAL QUIZ NO. 53

How well do you know the dumb criminal mind?

A man was sentenced to ninety days in jail for disorderly conduct, a fairly minor offense that carried a fairly minor sentence. While he was in jail did he . . .

- (a) take a matchbook correspondence course in VCR repair?
- (b) whittle a replica of the White House to scale out of soap?
- (c) invent a straw that you could eat chili with?
- (d) plot and execute a difficult escape?

Answers (a), (b), or (c) could all be rationalized as a good use of his time, but a criminal in Rhode Island chose (d). For eighty-eight laborious days he toiled over his plans, and then he finally accomplished his feat. On the next-to-last day of his ninety-day sentence, he made good his escape—for about five minutes. He was then re-arrested and sentenced to eighteen months.

Jumpin' Jack Flasher

Just outside Little Rock, Arkansas, a known "flasher" was at it again. Jumpin' Jack, as he was called by the local police, would often get naked and do calisthenics at his apartment window across the street from the local bank. Not only were his exercise habits offensive to the people who worked in the bank; local merchants also complained that Jack's jumping was bad for business.

Now, Jack was bold and a little demented, but he wasn't stupid. He would always hide his face in some way or pull the blinds halfway so that he could only be seen from the waist down. These precautions made it more difficult for him to be identified (especially in light of the fact that the police don't hold naked lineups).

After receiving a number of complaints one day, the Little Rock Police Department sent over one of its best officers to investigate. As the detective knocked on Jack's door, he thought about how hard it was to prove cases like Jack's. Without a positive I.D., such situations quickly degenerate to "my word against yours." Our detective decided to take a different approach.

"All right, Jack, who have you got hiding in there with you?"

"I don't have anyone hiding in here!" Jack yelled angrily from behind the door.

"The girls over at the bank tell it differently. They say they saw someone sneaking in here a little earlier today."

Jack opened the door. "They're crazy," he said. "There hasn't been anyone in my apartment all day long except me. See for yourself."

The officer did. He saw it all, from Jack's head down to his toes. Jumpin' Jack was finally arrested for indecent exposure.

Beats the Hell out of Me

Marshal Larry Hawkins of Little Rock has his own story about Jumpin' Jack Flasher.

"I had a run-in with Jack myself once," Hawkins told one of our *America's Dumbest Criminals* writers. "One day I was patrolling the downtown area when this skinny little guy stops my car. It was Jumpin' Jack. From the looks of him, he'd been worked over pretty good by somebody who wasn't messin' around. His left eye had a huge mouse under it, his lip was split open, and his face was all red, with a couple of knots on his head as well. He just looked like hell."

"What happened to you?" Hawkins asked.

"I've been beat up," Jack mumbled through clenched jaws.

"I'll say you have. Who beat you up, Jack?"

"This woman down at the Laundromat," he confessed in obvious pain and embarrassment.

"A woman? A woman did this to you?"

Hawkins thought maybe Jack had mixed it up with his girlfriend or something. So he put Jack in the back seat of the squad car and drove to the Laundromat. Through the storefront windows, the men could see several women inside cleaning clothes.

"Jack, which one was it that beat you up?"

"I don't know," he muttered. "I didn't see her face."

"Wait a minute . . . let me get this straight. A woman in there beat you up, and you don't know which one did it?"

"I told you, I didn't see her face."

"All right. You wait here while I go in and try to find out what happened." So Hawkins walked into the place. One of the women addressed Hawkins, "Officer, we are so glad you're here. A man came in here about ten minutes ago, pulled his shirt up over his head, and then dropped his pants."

"He wasn't wearing any underwear, either!" added another woman.

"So what happened then?" Hawkins asked, smiling.

One of the women continued: "Then the man said, 'Hey girls, does this remind you of anything?' And Connie said, 'Yeah, it does—it looks like a penis, only smaller!' Then she reached out and grabbed him by the hair under his tee shirt and commenced to knock the hell out of him."

"Yeah," the officer admitted. "That much is obvious."

"His arms were up over his head in that shirt," the informant went on, "and he couldn't do nothin'. It was over in about thirty seconds." Then she added with some satisfaction, "You don't mess with Connie!"

She was right about that, too, Hawkins thought as he looked at a substantial woman in the corner nonchalantly folding some sheets. *I certainly wouldn't mess with Connie!*

Hawkins got back in the squad car and told Jack he was under arrest for exposing his privates in public.

"Well, what about that woman in there? Aren't you gonna do anything about her beatin' me up like this?"

"I thought you told me that you didn't see who did it," the officer said. "But if you want to go back in there and see if you can figure out who it was, I'll just wait here for you, Jack."

"Uhhh . . . no . . . that's okay. Let's just get out of here," Jack said. He kept staring through the window at Connie, who was still folding clothes.

"Fine with me, Jack," Hawkins said. "Let's go."

Insulated from Good Sense

A narcotics team had a house in Indiana surrounded. With warrants in hand, they entered the house and searched the premises. The man who was making most of the drug sales was nowhere to be found, but they knew he was in there somewhere. The house had been under surveillance for some time.

Finally, the search took the officers to the attic. The place looked deserted, just like the rest of the house. One officer then noticed the right cheek of a pair of blue jeans sticking out of a roll of fiberglass insulation. At this point, an officer armed with a shotgun loaded another round into the chamber of his gun, even though his gun was already loaded. He was counting on the ominous sound of a pump shotgun being loaded to bring the suspect out of hiding.

Suddenly, the fiberglass roll started shaking and moving around, and the suspect was hollering, "Don't shoot! Don't shoot! I'm coming out . . . I'm coming out!"

But it wasn't the loading of the shotgun that had

prompted our friend to acknowledge his presence. Before the police knew it, their suspect was out of the roll and scratching himself all over. Every square inch of exposed skin was painfully red and inflamed from exposure to the fiberglass, and the suspect was so caught up in his scratching that he barely glanced at the cops. "I was ready to give up anyway," he mumbled.

That was one time a suspect was caught red-handed and red-faced . . . just itching to give himself up!

Suddenly, the fiberglass roll started shaking and moving around, and the suspect was hollering, "Don't shoot! Don't shoot! I'm coming out . . . I'm coming out!"

41

13 Going out with a Bang

Kerry and David weren't very nice people. Their idea of a good time was to get drunk and drive some thirty miles outside their southwestern city and wreak havoc on whatever innocent desert creatures happened across their paths. Mainly coyotes.

From their new four-by-four Blazer, they would either run them down or shoot them, or both, leaving their mangled carcasses lying in the desert. Sometimes they even set traps for the unsuspecting creatures, ensuring themselves sufficient victims for a day of demented sport.

Yes, the whole thing was sickening and deplorable. But there finally came a day when one small coyote managed to get in a little payback.

Our two sickos had removed a coyote from their trap and taped two sticks of dynamite to its body. Then they lit the fuses and turned the coyote loose.

Scared, confused, and panicked, the hapless creature ran . . . for about ten feet. Then it turned and ran straight back toward its tormentors, the lit dynamite still hissing at its side. Kerry and David ran. The coyote followed. It would rush one way, zig and zag, then chase after the other guy. Finally, the coyote ran for the nearest cover, which was a five-by-eleven-foot shaded area—right under the new Blazer.

The situation had quickly turned from bad to worse. The terrible two were now the ones scared, confused, and panicked. And they, like their little victim, were helpless. They couldn't chase him off. They couldn't drag him out. They couldn't even get near him. In fact, they had to run even faster now . . .

Kaboom! Bye-bye, Blazer.

Dumbfounded, the two ghoulies were suffering the consequences of their evil. They were thirty miles from home and stranded in the middle of the desert. No guns, no beer, no water, no whatever else they had brought with them—not to mention the loss of a twenty-thousand-dollar vehicle.

When the two were finally rescued and the investigation completed, the two faced charges of animal cruelty and other violations against nature. And once the truth was out, the insurance company refused to cover the Blazer.

It wasn't enough. But that little coyote, although doomed, had at least managed to give them a small taste of what they deserved.

14 A Large Naked Anchovy and Pepperoni

Police in Indiana arrested a man after an odd crime spree. It seems he dreamed of being a pizza delivery boy, so he decided he'd audition for the part. Police got the call when he went through an entire apartment complex knocking on doors—without a pizza, and wearing only a baseball cap.

Police arriving on the scene gave chase, and the would-be delivery man fled, only to injure himself as he attempted to jump over a fence. He was, shall we say, arrested and booked in thirty minutes . . . or less.

"Not by the Hair of My Chinny-Chin-Chin!"

Charlie Hackett, chief of police in Kokomo, Indiana, tells this story about dumb criminals determined to live high on the hog:

"Someone called in a complaint about some rustling going on out in the country. My partner and I were working organized crime at the time, but we were the only ones on duty, so we had to go. We found that this farmer had been losing big time—twenty-five or thirty hogs in all—but not all at once. Those hogs had been disappearing one at a time, one a night. And each time the rustlers had managed to take the whole pig. The farmer had found blood, but no carcasses."

Hackett and his partner staked out the area the next night. Before long, they saw a big station wagon rolling down a little lane near the hog pens. Three or four men got out. The officers used night lenses to watch the suspects walk down the lane toward the hog pens. Then the commotion started.

"They were running," Hackett remembers, "and the hogs were running. Then one of the guys pulled out a .22-caliber rifle and popped one of the hogs. He shot again, and the hog went down.

"Well, we backed off at that point, knowing they would have to come back down the lane with the hog they had shot. So we're sitting there waiting for them to get onto the highway so we can stop them. Sure enough, they came zipping down. We pulled them over."

The two officers approached the vehicle and peered inside, expecting to catch the rustlers red-handed. But all they saw were two men in the front seat, three men in the back—and no sign of a recently deceased hog.

One of the officers peered into the rear of the station wagon. "Nothing back there but an old seat," he said. Then they looked more closely and realized it was the backseat of the station wagon. The officers asked the men in the backseat to get out.

"Now, it didn't look too bad," Hackett says. "There was a seat cover over what appeared to be the backseat. One of our guys reached in and pulled off the cover."

It wasn't a seat at all. It was a very large, very dead hog. "We don't know how they did it, how they got that hog into the backseat—it must have weighed around five hundred pounds."

But that's not the end of our little pig tale.

Those hogs had been disappearing one at a time, one a night.

"Later on, we got a search warrant to go back to the house where one of these guys lived, and we found a small, live pig this guy had previously taken. We kept her for evidence, and one of our officers took her home to keep for the trial. By the time the trial came around, however, the officer had grown quite fond of the pig. He even had her paper-trained! The 'evidence' remained at the officer's home as a pet until she weighed about four hundred pounds, then she moved to a local farm."

Presumably, she never had to serve double duty as the backseat of a station wagon.

Junior Meets the Sandman

Officer Steve Turner of the Metropolitan Nashville Police Department had little trouble apprehending this tired, dumb criminal.

As homeowner Loretta Davin placed the last suitcase in the trunk of her car, she had no idea she was being watched. Twenty-six-year-old Fred "Junior" Williams, a small-time house burglar with a keen eye for opportunity, had been observing Davin for twenty minutes or so. Junior knew she was about to leave, and from the amount of luggage she was taking, he knew she would probably be gone for at least a couple days. Junior smiled as the car pulled out of the driveway, turned the corner at the end of the street, and disappeared.

Breaking in through a side door unnoticed was easy for our burglar. That's what he did for a living. And with the homeowner safely out of the way, this promised to be a stress-free operation.

Ah, life is good, thought Junior as he shook a pillow from its case. He then began a leisurely stroll through the house, filling his pillowcase with whatever he decided to take. There was some jewelry, some cash hidden under the mattress, the VCR—yes, life was good. This job was a piece of cake.

Hmmm . . . piece of cake. That sounded pretty good to Junior. He hadn't had lunch, and by now he had worked up quite an appetite rifling through the house. He decided to see what the kitchen had to offer.

Well, all right! The lady of the house hadn't bothered to clean out the fridge before she left. Junior found some nice chicken salad and a loaf of bread, a few carrot sticks, some potato chips, and some chocolate milk. *Hey, may as well put it on a tray, kick back, and catch a little TV.*

So that's just what Junior did. He carried the tray to the nightstand next to the bed, climbed in, clicked on the tube, and ate his lunch. But after all that hard work and that good meal, the bed was just too comfortable. The sandman came a-callin' on Junior, and soon he was out like a light.

Meanwhile, Loretta Davin had arrived at her office and learned that her business trip had been postponed. After being gone only three hours instead of three days, she returned home to find her side door broken open. Gripped with fear, she phoned the police from her car phone.

Turner was one of the first officers to arrive on the scene. Here's how he described it:

"As we entered the home, it was obvious that a burglary had occurred. Drawers were pulled out, closet doors stood wide open, and the place looked as if it had been ransacked. With weapons drawn, we cleared each room. As we got near the bedroom, I could hear voices, so we approached very cautiously. The television was still on. And there, all sprawled out, lay Junior, sleeping like he was in his own bed. The tray was there on the nightstand with some food still left on it, and the pillowcase of loot was sitting next to it.

"What a picture! We had had dealings with Junior before, so we all knew who he was. So we just kind of quietly encircled the bed and yelled, on cue, 'Junior! Wake up!' He did, and the look on his face was hysterical. We arrested him and took him to jail for breaking and entering, burglary, and sleeping on the job!"

Junior's short nap turned into a long stretch.

 **Write On!**

"I've got another story for you," Detective Ted Mc-Donald told us at a recent barbecue for *America's Dumbest Criminals* personnel in Brunswick, Georgia. "Adam Watson and I had to serve a warrant for cashing a stolen check on a man that lived here in Brunswick. I remember it because of the heat that day. It must have been a hundred. In fact, it was so hot that I saw two dogs fighting over a tree."

He smiled.

"As we arrived at the man's house and began to go up on the front porch, a dog starts barking. About this time a man comes from around the back of the house to see what the dog is barking at. It was us."

"Robert Norton?" the officers asked the man.

"Yeah, I'm Robert Norton. What can I do for you guys?"

"Mr. Norton, we have a warrant for your arrest for receiving and cashing a stolen check."

"Nah . . . you've got the wrong man." he said, shaking his head. "I never cashed a stolen check in my life. What makes you guys think I did something like that?"

"Well sir," Officer McDonald said, holding up the canceled check from the bank. "You forged the name the check was in on the front. But on the back, when you endorsed it, you signed your *real* name. And you provided the teller with your driver's license, complete with your current address."

"You weren't thinking too clearly at that moment, were you?" Watson asked.

"Let me see that check," the man said. He looked it over pretty good, front and back. Then he shook his head in disbelief and frustration.

"I'd never done anything like this before," he told the two detectives. "I guess when she asked me for my I.D. I just went into check-cashing mode. I can't believe I did that . . . pretty dumb, huh?"

"Pretty dumb," the officers echoed in unison. "Let's go."

 **Go Directly to Jail**

It was a late Thursday afternoon in a Florida panhandle locale when two young off-duty detectives in plain clothes were approached by a local drug dealer as they sat and talked over a cup of coffee. Not only were they off the clock; they were also out of their jurisdiction, just on the other side of the county line.

"S'up dudes?" the dealer bantered.

"Not much, man. What's up with you?"

"Ain't no thang. Y'all looking for a little somethin' for tonight?"

"Might be," the detectives answered. "Depends on what we find."

"Well, look no further—the Candy Man's here," he announced with pride of title on his face. "How's two hundred dollars sound for an eight ball?" (An eight ball is 3.5 grams of cocaine.)

"That sounds real good if it's the right thing."

"Oh, it's the right thing all right. That's why they call me the Candy Man, 'cause my deals are so sweet!"

"Sounds good," one of the officers repeated. "In fact, we'd probably want to do a couple of eight balls right now, only at the moment we don't have that much cash with us. But if we could take a little ride over to our office, I could get some money out of the safe."

"Not a problem," the Candy Man offered. "I need to go and see my boy to pick up some more anyway. Y'all can ride with me." So the two officers got into the Candy Man's car and rode with him to secure the drugs. After the pickup, the officers started giving Candy Man directions to their office.

After a half-dozen lefts and rights, the three arrived in front of their "office."

"Well, here we are, Candy Man." The officers smiled.

"This ain't no office building, man. This is the police station."

"That's right," they assured him. "We're cops."

"Aw, man . . . you guys are the law?"

"'Fraid so," the officers answered. "And you're under arrest for sale of a controlled substance."

"Damn." The Candy Man just hung his head and sighed. "And I was beginning to like you guys."

It's like your mother always told you. It doesn't pay to talk to strangers.

 # It's the Law

In Sweden, it's illegal to drive on the highway if you have the flu—because reaction time of people with the flu tested below those with alcohol in their systems.

Here, we have convictions for D.U.I.—"Driving under the Influence."

Are sickly Swedes in danger of being charged with D.U.W.—"Driving Under the Weather"?

He Can Hide, but He Can't Run

Terry Jarnigan was a troublemaker. He was always having brushes with the law, and he was especially well known for starting fights and somehow managing to get away just before the police arrived.

One Friday night Terry tried to pick up another man's wife in a local tavern in a Midwest town, and a fight ensued. Soon the whole place was involved in an old-fashioned barroom brawl, with chairs and glasses being thrown and broken amidst a frenzied free-for-all.

Then someone yelled "Cops!" The crowd broke for the door, and Jarnigan was one of the first ones out. But the squad car pulled in, lights flashing, just as he was making his way across the parking lot. With no time to think and few places to run, Jarnigan opened the door of a brown Pontiac Bonneville and stretched out along the back floorboard.

In a matter of minutes, more officers and squad cars had pulled into the parking lot. Jarnigan would have to sit tight for a while. He just lay there in the back of the Pontiac, watching the shadows of the flashing lights and listening to the voices outside. He couldn't hear everything that was said as the police began arresting the people involved in the donnybrook. But he did hear his own name over and over as bar patrons explained the origins of the fight.

Then Terry Jarnigan heard voices coming closer to his hiding place.

"It's not fair to arrest me!" a man was protesting in a shrill voice. "I didn't start the fight. Some jerk was hitting on my wife, and she didn't like it. Well, I didn't like it either, so I just . . . "

"Yes, sir," another voice answered calmly. "We'll get all of that sorted out down at the police station. But we don't have any more room in the cruisers, so you'll have to follow me downtown in your own vehicle."

"He's the one you ought to be arresting . . . " The man was still muttering as he swung open the door of his brown Pontiac Bonneville. Terry Jarnigan blinked as the dome light came on, and the car's owner jumped back and yelled.

"Hey! Here he is—here's the punk that started the whole thing! You just wait till I get my . . . "

The officer stopped the furious husband just before he took hold of the cowering troublemaker. Jarnigan was duly booked for inciting a riot and for committing illegal trespass in entering the man's car. And then he was thrown into the same holding tank with the people he had provoked into fighting in the bar only an hour earlier, including the enraged husband of the woman he had flirted with.

They were all very glad to see him.

Lovin' in Fifteen Minutes

Is speeding a crime of passion? Officer Rusty Martin remembers a time when the label could have applied.

"I was a rookie stationed in a little town called Duncan, Mississippi," Martin says. "Now, nothing much ever happened in Duncan. The nights were even quieter than the days, and I was working the 6:00 P.M. to 3:00 A.M. shift. So I was always looking for ways to liven up those long hours."

One night Martin, who lived about thirty miles on the other end of the county, was headed home down the dark, quiet country lanes. He was in a hurry to get home and had already exceeded the speed limit when he noticed headlights in the distance behind him, closing in fast. Martin didn't have radar at that time, so he tried to pace the car behind him.

"I clicked it up to about eighty in order to get an indication of how fast he was going. Sure enough, he caught up with me easily. Then he saw the bar lights on my squad car and slammed on his brakes."

The late-night speedster climbed out of his car and read the officer's badge. "Please Officer Martin!" he begged. "You can't write me a ticket. I can't afford it—I just can't afford the ticket. Please just let me off with a warning."

It was very late. Martin was bored and just a little punchy, so he decided to have some fun. "I'll tell you what I'll do," he said. "If you can give me an excuse I haven't heard before, I won't write you this ticket."

The speedster didn't hesitate. "I left home about five o'clock this afternoon, and I told my wife, 'Honey, I won't be gone long.' Well, I got down to Mount Bayou, and we got to gambling, and I lost most of my money, so I had to stay until I could win some of it back."

Martin just nodded, pen in hand.

"Then my wife called," the speeder continued. "She said, 'There's going to be a whole lot of lovin' going on in this house in fifteen minutes, and if you want to be in on it, you had better be here.' That was fourteen minutes ago, and I'm trying my best to get there."

"The man wasn't joking," Martin remembers. "And I had to admit I never heard that one before. I let him go. What happened after that is anybody's guess."

Look Out! He's Got a Turtle and He Knows How to Use It!

It was a classic case of love gone wrong in Indiana. Boy meets girl. Boy falls in love. Girl doesn't.

In this case, she really did try to let him down easy, but he was distraught. He was fuming as he barreled out of her kitchen door and into the night.

The brokenhearted Romeo staggered through the fields in the throes of lover's angst. Then he saw his weapon, seized it, and started back to his girlfriend's house.

In a rage, Romeo returned and chased his ex-girlfriend around the kitchen with a large snapping turtle. He was much faster than Juliet and he easily caught her in the small kitchen, but he couldn't get the turtle to bite her. Finally, Juliet managed to call the police. The officers

He was much faster than Juliet and he easily caught her in the small kitchen, but he couldn't get the turtle to bite her.

arrived, disarmed (deturtled?) the irate lover, and arrested him for assault with a reptile.

The incident marked the definite end of one relationship, but the beginning of another. Juliet thought the big turtle was cute, and she was ever so grateful that he hadn't bitten her. The girl and the turtle are still together and living happily in Pennsylvania, according to the policeman who retold the story.

Luck of the Draw

With Oregon State Lottery ticket in hand, Alice Krumm stood staring at the winning numbers posted on the cash register. So close . . . but not quite. The ticket she had just bought was only one digit away from the twenty-dollar winning number. For once in her life, Alice wanted to be a winner instead of a near-miss.

Alice struggled with her greed for a long minute before finally giving in. Creeping around behind the baked beans and canned goods, she altered her lottery ticket with a ballpoint pen to win the twenty dollars, then returned to the counter to collect her ill-gotten prize.

But she should have worked a little harder on her forgery. The clerk spotted it immediately and called the police. The dishonest lottery player was arrested on the spot and charged with fraud.

Then the arresting officer made an interesting discovery. He found the real number under her bad forgery. His revelation made her feel even dumber.

Had she looked farther up the chart of winning numbers, she would have discovered that her original ticket number had also been a winner—for five thousand dollars!

Pulling the Rug Out

In Peoria, Illinois, police were called to the scene of a home burglary. The perplexed homeowners reported that the house had indeed been burglarized, but that none of the normal things were missing. The television and VCR were still there, although each had been moved a little. A stereo system, jewelry, and even some cash all could be accounted for. It turned out that only one major item was missing—but it was a significant one. An entire houseful of new wall-to-wall carpet had been taken up and stolen.

The officers on the scene were as perplexed as the burglary victims. They really had no idea how to track a hot carpet. Scratching their heads, they headed outside into the newly fallen snow to look around.

But wait! What's this? In the yard, footprints showed on either side of a long, scraped trail leading out toward a nearby field. Either the carpet had been dragged in that direction, or a brontosaurus had just strolled by.

The officers followed the trail across the yard, through the field, and into another yard, where the trail ended at a neighbor's front door.

When the police entered the small home behind a larger main house, they found not a brontosaurus, but the stolen carpet on the floor—recut and laid to fit its new home. The young man who lived there insisted that he had purchased the rug, but the police showed him his own trail from the "carpet store." He was arrested and charged with the crime.

Don't Try It Again, Sam

In Thibodaux, Louisiana, a blundering, wannabe robber with speech difficulties just couldn't win for losing. Sam Lincoln entered Bob's Cafe and, speaking in his thick, backwoods Cajun accent, ordered the waitress to "give me all the money."

Unfortunately, she couldn't understand a word he said. To her it sounded like he was ordering "a sieve with all the honey."

In desperation, Sam turned to a patron and told him to hand over all *his* money. The diner could have sworn that Sam said to "live a big pile of bunny."

When the patron couldn't understand him either, Sam got so frustrated that he pulled out his gun. Now they would hear the unmistakable voice of his thirty-eight.

Sam pulled the trigger.

Click.

The gun wouldn't fire.

Now Sam grabbed the cash register and began to run. But he didn't get far—only about three feet. The register was still firmly plugged into the wall, and he quickly ran out of cord.

The register was jerked out of Sam's hands, and he fell. Humiliated and frustrated, he ran out of Bob's Cafe empty-handed. Waitresses and patrons breathed a sigh of relief. Someone hefted the register back up to its place on the counter.

But five minutes later, Sam was back. This time, he made sure he unplugged the register before making off with it. Sam was ecstatic—for about three feet. A by-stander who had witnessed the whole comedy of errors knocked Sam down and made a citizen's arrest.

Bound for the Cooler

26

One bright spring morning in Lafayette, Louisiana, Louis Albright had the bright idea of robbing a branch of a local bank. Louis had an even more brilliant idea for a low-cost, low-fat, completely disposable disguise. He would cover his entire head with whipped cream.

A few trial runs indicated his idea would work beautifully. The foamy "mask" sprayed on quickly and was easily wiped off. It completely covered any distinguishing marks, even his hair color. And it tasted wonderful, to boot.

Congratulating himself on his innovative idea, the human hot-fudge sundae walked into the bank and approached the teller. Unfortunately, the employees' response to his delicious disguise was just the opposite of what he wanted. The giggles were discreet at first, but when he said, "Put all your money in the sack," the giggles dissolved into open laughter.

By this time the whipped cream was getting warm and beginning to slide. And the teller had long ago punched the silent alarm. Before you could say "banana split," the police arrived. The rapidly melting bank robber was quickly arrested and refrigerated downtown.

By this time the whipped cream was getting warm and beginning to slide. And the teller had long ago punched the silent alarm.

Two-Bit Thief

Rhode Island police were sure they had the right man when the suspect charged with a string of vending-machine robberies paid his four-hundred-dollar bail entirely in quarters.

A Really Big Bust

At first, the customs officer thought the drug-sniffing dog was barking up the wrong tree. Or, rather, sniffing up the wrong tourist.

As the 475-pound man waddled through customs, the dog began to pay him close attention, sniffing suspiciously at the man's huge stomach. Annoyed, the man told the dog to "shoo." No luck.

The customs officer was a bit reluctant to approach the man, since he really didn't fit the profile of a smuggler, and his personal effects had already been examined. But the dog was relentless. Over and over it pointed its nose toward the tourist and kept sniffing and whining and sniffing. It was almost as though the dog itself was puzzled.

The officer finally conceded that something was awry.

"I'm sorry, sir," he told the rotund tourist. "I'm afraid you're going to have to accompany me to a dressing room for a strip search."

It was a task that neither man was looking forward to. But it had to be done.

Once inside the room, the tourist was ordered to disrobe, and a complete body search was initiated. It was then that a plastic bag containing eleven ounces of a white powdery substance was discovered—discreetly hidden amid the many folds of the man's tremendous stomach!

The substance proved to be cocaine.

The drug dog was vindicated.

Bare Truth

In a small town in Texas late on a Saturday afternoon, a small mom-and-pop store was robbed by a lone gunman. The prime suspect was quickly spotted. In fact, everybody in town spotted him. They didn't even need a detailed description. The fleeing felon was running down the street completely naked.

But Ted Jowers had a great alibi ready for the police officers who stopped him. "I like to get in touch with nature when I jog," he told them.

Somehow, though, Ted didn't seem like the nature type—or the jogging type, for that matter. The officers brought him in.

Ted finally broke down and confessed to the robbery. Then he explained to the police that he had stripped down to streak away after the robbery because he thought his clothes would make him more identifiable.

Ah, the ironic naked truth of the dumb criminal plan.

30 Love Thy Neighbor

The weary, disheveled woman tossed and turned in her bed. It was two in the morning, and the trucks at the nearby warehouse were grinding their gears, braking loudly, and making that maddening "Beep! Beep! Beep!" sound that a postal truck makes when in reverse gear.

What is so important that you have to truck it in the middle of the night? she wondered.

Finally, the unwilling insomniac could stand no more. She called the police and complained about the noise.

A quick check downtown revealed that the warehouse was leased to a toy import company. That set the officers to wondering. Christmas was still many months away. Why would a toy company be working round the clock to ship Chinese dolls and robots that spew smoke?

Ten minutes later, the two officers who had been sent to follow up on the disturbing-the-peace complaint pulled their cruiser up behind the working docks. When they stepped out of their vehicle, the men on the loading dock scattered and disappeared into the night.

The officers figured they must have a burglary in progress and called for backup. Three of the men were quickly apprehended in the neighborhood, but they turned out to be the rightful occupants of the warehouse.

So why had they fled?

Well, they weren't burglars, but they were guilty of a bit more than disturbing the peace. The police searched the warehouse and ended up seizing twenty-two tons of cocaine, with a street value of more than six billion dollars.

It was the biggest drug raid in U.S. history, and it carries a lesson for all would-be dumb criminals: If you're going to mess with Uncle Sam, make sure you don't wake up the neighbors!

DUMB CRIMINAL QUIZ NO. 007

How well do you know the dumb criminal mind?

An officer fired at a bearded burglary suspect. The fleeing felon was unhurt, but the bullet tore a hole in the man's shirt as it flapped in the breeze. The criminal escaped. Immediately afterward, did he . . .

(a) sew his shirt while he watched television?
(b) shave his beard and go right down to the police station?
(c) use his shirt as a hand puppet to entertain children?
(d) try and take his shirt back for a refund?

If your answer was (b), you are correct. In Atlanta, a burglar was fired at by officers, escaped unhurt, and returned to his own home. When he got home, he quickly shaved his beard to fool the police and then went right to the police station to report that his car had been stolen. He was arrested on the spot.

Why? First, in his haste, he had cut himself shaving, so his face was a bloody mess. Oh, and he also forgot to change the shirt that had the bullet hole in it.

Five Will Get You Ten or Twenty-Five

With a long sigh, Janice Patterson finished writing her check on her account and received the five-dollar bill from the bank teller. She actually needed more, but her balance was far too low at the moment. She wouldn't get her next paycheck for two more days. Until then, she would just have to get by on those five dollars.

Janice got into her car, swung the door shut, and put the key in the ignition. Just as she was starting the engine, a man jumped in the front seat beside her and pointed a gun right at her face. "Give me all your money—right now!" he demanded in a harsh voice.

Reluctantly, but obediently, Janice turned over her five-dollar bill.

"It's all I have," she explained.

"You're kidding!" The bad guy put the gun down. Incredulous, he searched her purse and the glove compartment before he finally realized she was telling the truth.

"Damn—wouldn't you know it! All those people

comin' out of the bank, and I have to pick the one that don't got no money!"

All Janice could do was shrug. But now her would-be robber decided to take a different approach. "Write me a check!" he ordered.

But Janice had to shrug again. She had just written the last of the checks in her checkbook.

Obviously, this was not going well at all for our criminal.

"I gotta think!" he mused, then ordered her to drive around the block. Janice obeyed.

They had just turned the corner when another problem apparently occurred to the worried criminal. His victim had seen what he looked like and presumably could relay his description to the police.

"Don't look at me," he warned. "You keep looking at the floor, hear me?"

"That would be difficult," she told the crook. "I'm driving, remember?"

"Well, you just look straight ahead. Don't look at me." She didn't.

Momentarily frustrated, the bandit then remembered that banks keep counter checks available for customer use. He directed his victim to drive back to the bank.

They went inside to one of the desks, where he directed her to write a check for eighty-five dollars. She didn't bother to tell him she didn't have that much in the account. But she did try to communicate with the teller. As the bandit fidgeted and glanced around, Janice gestured, mimed, made faces, and even pointed at the man, but her dramatics had no effect on the teller.

Resigning herself to the victim's role, the woman handed the check to the bandit, but in her nervousness she neglected to sign it.

The teller, finally tipped of by the omission of the signature, slipped back to the manager's office, where a call was made to police. The robber was arrested, convicted, and sentenced to ten years in jail.

Janice Patterson barely escaped punishment herself.

"It's a good thing you didn't sign it," the teller pointed out to her. "The check would have bounced, and we would have had to charge you a twenty-five-dollar processing fee."

Big Mac Attackers

Retired Officer David Hunter of the Knox County (Tennessee) Sheriff's Department tells this story of two very hungry holdup men:

After an evening of partying and smoking dope, the two very high potheads decided they would kill two birds with one stone. They were broke, and they had the "munchies," so they agreed that the best thing to do would be to rob a hamburger joint. Armed with loaded shotguns, they burst through the door of the first place they came upon.

"Give us all the money," the dim-bulb duo demanded, "and a dozen hamburgers with everything—to go!"

"I'll get you the money, man," one frightened employee replied, "but the grill's already been shut down. It'll take about ten minutes to reheat."

"Do it," came the gunman's reply. "We'll wait!"

Meanwhile, a passing motorist noticed that the two

men sitting in the burger shack were holding shotguns. Suspicious indeed. The motorist phoned police.

"Here's your food," the shaking worker said.

The burger bandits grabbed the greasy sack and hit the door just as the sound of police sirens and squealing tires filled the night air. In their haste, they left the stolen money sitting on the table.

Panicked, the two robbers ran across a highway, slid down an embankment, and tried to hide under a bridge, which is where the K-9 unit found them. The hamburger heist was over.

"What really pisses me off," one man said to the other as they were being led away in handcuffs, "is that those damn dogs ate all our burgers. I didn't even get one bite!"

The officer responded, "You ought to be glad those are the only buns the dog bit."

 # In the Mood

Trooper Robert Bell shared this story of true romance at a very tender age in the Southeast:

Bell was headed out to the interstate highway through a small town when he noticed a classic car whipping by at a high rate of speed. It was a '64 Buick in mint condition. Radar revealed the vehicle was traveling at fifty miles per hour—*over* the speed limit.

When Bell closed in on the Buick, the speeder acted as if he might force a chase, but then he abruptly pulled over. Bell approached the idling Buick carefully. When he got to the window, he saw that the driver was an elderly man who appeared to be quite agitated.

"Sir," the trooper said, "were you aware that you were doing eighty-five in a thirty-five-mile-per-hour zone?"

"Of course I know how fast I'm going," the driver snapped. "It's an emergency!"

Concerned, the officer asked, "Is it a medical emergency, sir? I can get you to a hospital."

The driver's face reddened. "No, I have to go now. It's an emergency!"

"What's the emergency, sir? Maybe I can help you."

The old gentleman just looked angrier than ever. "I can't tell you. You'll laugh at me."

Bell tried to reassure him. "I won't laugh at you, sir. But if you don't tell me what the emergency is, I'll have to write you a ticket."

The senior speedster finally relented. "You promise not to laugh—man to man?" He was very serious.

"No, sir," Bell said. "I promise."

"Well, son, I'm eighty-two years old, and I haven't had an erec-uh . . . well, I haven't been 'in the mood for love' for more than two years now. Well, I have an—uh, I'm in the mood right now, and I'm on my way to my girl-friend's house!"

Bell was stunned, but only for a moment. "I had never heard that excuse for speeding before and—man to man—well, I had to empathize just a little. So I gave him a police escort."

There's One Born Every Minute

Circus man P. T. Barnum is famous for saying that there's a sucker born every minute. Retired captain Don Parker of the Escambia County Sheriff's Department in Pensacola, Florida, reports an unusual incident that proves Mr. Barnum's point:

A resident of a quiet neighborhood was walking his dog in the woods one evening when the animal sniffed out a woman's purse. The man unzipped the purse to look for identification. Instead of a wallet, a comb, or a lipstick, he found several curious packages, about the size of small bricks, wrapped in plastic and sealed with duct tape. Suspicious, he called the cops.

A patrolling deputy soon arrived and took the purse and its contents back to the station. As suspected, the packages contained drugs—pure cocaine with an estimated street value of two hundred thousand dollars.

The narcotics division immediately set up surveillance at the site where the purse had been found, hoping that someone would try to retrieve the drugs. But there was no activity, even though the officers stayed until well after midnight. Finally, as they were about to give up, one of them had a brilliant idea.

"Give me a piece of paper," he whispered to his partner. Then he wrote, "I found your purse and the contents. Call me. Large reward expected." He listed one of the confidential phone numbers that bypassed the department's switchboard and rang directly in the narcotics office.

The narcotics officer quickly taped the note to a stick and placed it where the purse had been. Then he and his partner went home.

The narcotics officers' fellow workers were highly amused the next morning when they learned about the note. For the rest of the day, the two were teased unmercifully. But the jokes stopped abruptly when they got a call around three in the afternoon.

A female cop answered the phone and set the trap. She demanded ten thousand dollars in cash for the safe return of the purse and its contents. At first the person on the other end of the line balked, but she made it clear he would have to pay up if he wanted the dope back. Finally, he agreed.

The drop was set for a phone booth outside the local mall. Undercover deputies took up positions in the parking lot around the booth.

The male and female narcotics officers stood by the phone booth, the female cop holding the purse. Soon a car with three occupants pulled up.

One suspect got out of the car and handed the narcotics officers a shopping bag that was bulging with cash. The female undercover officer gave the suspect the purse, and the man turned to go back to his car. That's when the cops got the drop on the suspects.

When both cops drew their weapons, the suspect started to go for his own, but thought better of it. Seeing that his friend was in trouble, the driver of the car did what had to be done—he prepared to save his own tail. Before he could get the car in gear, however, he found himself staring down the gun barrels of about a dozen policemen.

The final score was six pounds of cocaine, ten thousand dollars in cash, three suspects arrested, one car confiscated, and a nice leather purse. And the bust might never have been made if that one narcotics officer hadn't posted the sign.

It just goes to show: There *is* a sucker born every minute. And it always pays to advertise.

The Sad Saga of Bad Luck Brown

Don Parker of Pensacola also has a string of tales to tell about a dumb criminal who richly earned his nickname of Bad Luck Brown.

"We called him that because this guy had atrocious luck," Parker remembers. "Plus he wasn't all that bright. He was a small-time crook who spent more time in jail than he did out.

"I think the first time I met Bad Luck was in 1978 when I rolled in on a robbery call at a church on Sunday morning during the sermon. Bad Luck had robbed the collection plate. He made good on his escape and got away clean with all the cash, but he dropped his wallet. All we had to do was check his driver's license, then go by his house and pick him up."

But the dumbest crime Bad Luck Brown ever committed was one of his unluckiest, too.

There had been a string of motel robberies in the Pensacola area, and the police had received a tip on where the motel thieves were going to hit next. They always hit the motels around midnight, and the cops planned to be ready for them. Officers were stationed in the motel office and in parked cars around the parking lot. Parker was in the woods across the street with three other officers.

Just past midnight, an old, beat-up station wagon slowly passed the motel. It rattled up the road, turned around, and came back. The vehicle didn't fit the description of the motel robbers, and there was only one person in the car. But the motel thieves might have changed cars, or they might have just been casing the place. All the hidden officers watched it carefully.

The car turned around and came back for a third pass. Don Parker called his sergeant across the street on his walkie-talkie. "You think this might be our guys?"

"Nah, but he sure is interested in something."

The car stopped, a door opened, the driver leaned out and looked around cautiously. The sergeant wasn't taking any chances.

"All units stand by. We've got some activity out here, but I don't know what's going on."

Everybody watched as the mystery man stepped from the car.

"He's on the ground." The man walked around his vehicle and into the light of a street lamp. "He's on the

But Bad Luck Brown's luck held true. Just as he was about to disappear, he tripped over one of the officers and sprained his ankle.

street side of his car now. Okay, I can see him now . . . oh, no!'

Parker didn't like the tone of Sarge's voice. "What? What?"

Sarge radioed back, "It's Bad Luck Brown."

The man eased over to the patch of grass in front of the motel and finally stopped next to a lawn mower that someone had carelessly left out.

Sarge was almost laughing. "I don't believe it. He's stealing the lawn mower!"

Quickly and silently, Bad Luck Brown rolled the lawn mower to his station wagon, dropped the tailgate, and loaded the mower into his car.

"Move in." Sarge gave the command with a bit of resigned frustration in his voice.

The two unmarked cars in the parking lot pulled up to block the station wagon just as Bad Luck started it up. The officers hopped out with drawn guns and called him to freeze. Instead, Bad Luck jumped out and made a run for it. He dashed across the street into the woods—right where Parker was hiding.

"We almost scared him to death when we jumped out. But he was determined to get away this time, so he bolted to the left into the dense undergrowth. Now, a foot chase at night in the woods is the worst. You're running into trees and falling down into gullies. So I decided to try to scare him into stopping.

"'Halt, or I'll shoot!' I fired my gun into the ground. Unfortunately, this didn't have the effect I had hoped for. All the officers hit the ground, but Bad Luck just sped up. It looked like he was going to get away clean."

But Bad Luck Brown's luck held true. Just as he was about to disappear, he tripped over one of the officers and sprained his ankle.

"We never did see the motel thieves that night," Parker says. "But once again, it was our privilege to book Bad Luck Brown. He never ceased to amaze us."

Another Run of Bad Luck Brown

Yet another story about the notorious Bad Luck Brown from Pensacola, Florida, involves a time when this dumb criminal's bad luck *almost* changed.

One sunny afternoon Bad Luck Brown entered a busy liquor store with the intent of robbing it. Once he got into the store, however, there were too many people around for a real stickup, so he switched to Plan B. Fishing in his pocket for a piece of paper, Bad Luck scrawled a note to the cashier demanding money.

The cashier read the note and quickly handed over all the money in the drawer. In a flash, Bad Luck was out the door and gone. He seemed to have pulled off his robbery with flawless precision.

Except for one thing.

When the police arrived on the scene, they found the holdup note used in the robbery. When they turned it over, they knew exactly who to go after and where to find him.

Bad Luck Brown had written the note on the back of a letter he had received from his probation officer—complete with his name and address. When police tracked him down at home, they were able to inform him that his streak of bad luck was still intact.

This explosion, they believed, would pour millions of cubic feet of water onto the helpless city, transforming Nashville into a sort of country-and-western Atlantis.

A Dam Dumb Idea

In the great state of Tennessee three fools came up with a plan to make themselves rich. They were going to knock off the entire city of Nashville.

Our schemers needed a few supplies. Dynamite, for instance—lots of dynamite. Their warped plan was to blow up Percy Priest Dam approximately ten miles east of the city. This explosion, they believed, would pour millions of cubic feet of water onto the helpless city, transforming Nashville into a sort of country-and-western Atlantis. Then they would don their scuba gear, swim through the submerged city, and steal all the Rolexes, diamond rings, and money they could carry.

Bizarre, yes, but that was the plan. Our three aquatic airheads bought some dynamite, carried it to the dam, and succeeded in setting it off. The small explosion did little serious damage. The scheme wasn't even discovered until a short time later, when the explosive conspirators were captured and arrested.

38 **Arrest Record**

The record for being arrested belongs to Tommy Johns of Brisbane, Australia. By 1985, Tommy had been arrested for drunkenness two thousand times, according to Brisbane police. His total number of arrests for public drunkenness at the time of his death in 1988 was "nearly three thousand."

Legend has it that when Tommy was cremated, it took three weeks to put out the fire.

It's the Law

In the 1980s, New York's nonviolent offenders were allowed to choose sidewalk sweeping or trash collecting instead of jail time.

Of the first one hundred arrested, ninety-seven chose jail time!

They all knew that jail was safer than the sidewalks of New York City—probably cleaner, too.

The Light at the End of the Tennie

Just outside Lawrence, Kansas, police were called to an all-night market that had just been robbed. A male Caucasian had brandished a weapon and demanded money from a store employee. After stuffing the money into his pants pocket, he fled down the street.

Units in the area responded quickly to the alarm. Within moments, two officers on patrol had spotted a man running behind some houses in a nearby neighborhood. Certain that they had the right man, they gave chase on foot.

But the suspect wasn't really worried. It was dark, he was a very fast runner, and he knew the neighborhood like the back of his hand. He was sure he would have no trouble eluding the cops.

It didn't take long for the fleet-footed suspect to leave the first pair of officers behind, but he was surprised when more officers quickly joined in the chase. Each time the thief would elude one officer, he would be

The pursuing officers had just followed the lights.

spotted by another. The crook couldn't understand it; he was using his best moves.

At last there were too many officers on the scene who apparently could see quite well in the dark. Our suspect looked frustrated and surprised when he was finally captured.

But he was even more surprised and frustrated once the police told him how they knew where he was all the time. He really hadn't been hard to follow at all, thanks to advanced technology.

The pursuing officers had just followed the lights. Not the infrared lights used for night vision, but the red lights on the heels of the suspect's high-tech tennis shoes—the ones that blinked on and off every time his feet hit the ground.

Possession Is Nine-Tenths of the Law

In Edina, Minnesota, two would-be robbers hit on a foolproof getaway plan—or so they thought. Rather than using one of their own vehicles, which would be traced directly back to their home, they decided to steal a pickup truck right before they robbed the bank.

Two blocks from the bank, they found a really nice pickup easy to hot wire. They then parked their stolen pickup outside the Norton Bank while they went inside to rob it.

So far, so good. But those bandits hadn't figured on the determination of the pickup's owner, who had spotted them driving away and sprinted after them.

The two clever thieves got a substantial haul of money from the bank and then ran outside to find their stolen truck had been, well . . . stolen. The original owner had reclaimed it while they were busy at the bank. Panicked, the robbers attempted their getaway on foot, but they failed. The next pickup in this story was by the police.

The hapless robber finally made it to his truck with a fistful of greenbacks, only to have his car key break off in the door. As if that wasn't bad enough, he shot himself in the foot with his revolver while struggling to open the locked door.

All Thumbs

There are some days when nothing seems to go right—and this is truer of dumb criminals than it is of most of us.

Near Cleveland, Ohio, a lone gunman entered a cafe, pointed a gun at the waitress, and announced, "This is a robbery!" The waitress filled a paper bag with money as instructed, and the gunman escaped with the cash. But as the man ran across the parking lot the bag tore open, spilling bills and coins across the asphalt.

The hapless robber finally made it to his truck with a fistful of greenbacks, only to have his car key break off in the door. As if that wasn't bad enough, he shot himself in the foot with his revolver while struggling to open the locked door.

A few minutes later, he hobbled into a hospital emergency room. The police were notified and the footloose, clumsy, unlucky bandit was arrested.

What's the Number for 911?

Dumb criminals usually do their best to avoid arrest, but there are exceptions even to that rule. Charlie Hackett, chief of police in Kokomo, Indiana, remembers a criminal who decided the police were by far the lesser of the evils confronting him.

"There was a guy in town we'd had some problems with," Hackett recalls. "He was only about eighteen or nineteen years old, but he'd been arrested several times as a juvenile and was generally a troublemaker. And now he was wanted on a warrant for a burglary. So I was surprised when he called me on the phone at the station."

At the time, Hackett was a lieutenant working the detective division. His desk was in a large, busy room, and the room was so noisy he could hardly hear anything.

Hackett answered the phone and barely heard someone whispering, "Hello? Hello? Is this Lieutenant Hackett?"

The lieutenant put a hand over his other ear and shouted into the phone. "Could you speak up a little bit?"

"This is Joe Miller," whispered the voice on the other end.

"Joe, why are you being so quiet?" Lieutenant Hackett asked. Then he added, "We have a warrant for your arrest, you know."

"I know," Joe answered. "That's why I'm calling you . . . to turn myself in."

Over the phone, in the background, Hackett could hear a strange boom, boom, boom—like someone pounding on a door.

"C'mon Joe," he repeated, "speak up. I can't hear you."

"I can't talk very loud. I just wanted to turn myself in— come get me right away."

It turned out that an angry father and his son had caught Joe messing around with the man's daughter. Now they had Joe cornered in a room. One was at the front door, and one was at the back door. Turning himself in was just Joe's way of asking for police protection.

He figured—no doubt correctly—that almost any amount of jail time would be less painful than five minutes alone with that woman's father.

Backseat Driver

When police pull over a driver, they're always ready to hear the "big story." Sergeant Doug Baldwin of the Pensacola (Florida) Police Department remembers a time when a van was swerving and weaving across the center line. When the officer approached the van, now stopped, he noticed that the driver had moved over to the passenger's seat.

The officer shined his flashlight across the front seat to the man who had suddenly become the passenger in a driverless van. The officer asked for the man's driver's license and registration.

"I wasn't driving," the man claimed and pointed to the backseat. "The guy in the back was."

The officer shined his flashlight in back and got a good look at the perpetrator—a huge teddy bear.

It didn't take the officer long to assess the situation. One of the van's occupants was stuffed. The other was obviously loaded.

Door-to-Door Crime Buster

An officer in Savannah developed a bold but simple approach to drug busts. This uniformed patrolman would walk up to a known drug house or party and knock on the door. The occupant would answer the door with almost the same greeting every time. In fact, the similarity of the incidents was astounding. Each person reacted in almost the same manner every time the officer tried this very direct approach to crime busting. It went something like this:

Dumb Criminal opens door. "Uh . . . hello, officer. Is the music too loud? Did someone complain?"

"Nah, I just wanted to buy a bag of dope."

"Huh?"

"Do you have a bag of dope I can buy?"

"Well . . . but you're a cop."

"So? Can't I buy a bag of dope?"

"But . . . "

"Hey, I'm cool, okay?"

"Cool. Wait right here."

A minute later, the dumb (and about-to-be arrested) criminal would be selling the uniformed officer a bag of dope.

The bold officer made so many arrests this way that he was promoted to detective in record time. Almost all of his arrests were pleaded out without a trial because the criminals didn't want to admit in court they had sold drugs to a uniformed cop at their own apartment.

Drag Race

It was another routine day on patrol at a shopping mall. Officer Dusty Cutler had just grabbed a quick lunch and returned to her squad car when she saw a blond woman sprint out the mall entrance and into the parking lot.

"She was an attractive woman," Cutler remembers. "She wore a nice print dress, high heels . . . and she was very tall."

But why was she running? Seconds later Cutler got an answer when two men ran out the door and pursued the woman across the parking lot.

At first, Cutler thought the two men were harassing the woman. Then they got closer, and she heard them shouting, "Stop her! She robbed us!"

Cutler later learned that the woman had shoplifted women's clothing from a store in the mall and then assaulted one of the managers. The two men chasing her through the busy parking lot were the store's other manager and a salesclerk.

As the suspect ran in front of Cutler's car, she hiked up her dress in order to run faster, exposing a large pair of women's underwear. They were bulkier than normal, and Cutler could see a sleeve from a woman's blouse sticking out through the leg opening.

As the shoplifter sprinted away, the large baggy underwear stuffed with stolen merchandise slipped down over the suspect's thighs. At that point the officer noticed something extra that obviously didn't come from a store. The woman shoplifter, evidently, was not a woman.

By now the officer was having a difficult time calling in the report because she was laughing so hard. And the fleeing shoplifter was rapidly losing ground. With every step, the loaded underwear slipped farther down the suspect's legs. Finally, they fell to the ground and sent their wearer sprawling.

Still trying to make a graceful getaway, the fugitive scrambled back up, kicked off both the offending underwear and the high heels, and ran faster. But by this time Cutler had pulled the patrol car into the suspect's path, and the fleeing criminal slammed across the hood of the car. She/he was arrested and charged with shoplifting.

Cutler still speaks of that shoplifter-in-drag as the strangest criminal she ever—literally—ran into.

The woman had shoplifted women's clothing from a store in the mall and then assaulted one of the managers.

 **Bad Bribes**

A New York cop was working traffic one night when a muscular chap in a small car zipped right through a red light. When the officer pulled the vehicle over and made his approach, the driver immediately identified his occupation. The officer was interested, but not particularly impressed, to learn that the guilty motorist was a masseur. The officer was writing out the ticket when the masseur attempted to bribe the officer by offering him a massage.

He got the ticket anyway—perhaps because the whole experience just rubbed the officer the wrong way.

Colen
10/05

Type Ohhhhhhh!

When Charlie Beavers broke into a plasma center one Saturday night in Pensacola, Florida, he didn't get much —primarily because he didn't get too far.

Now, to a normal, rational mind, breaking into a plasma center might not make much sense. But to Charlie, it seemed like a good idea at the time. So after checking out the building, Charlie removed the top from an air vent on the roof and entered feet first. *Great*, he thought. *I'll just slide down this air vent, steal everything in sight, and make a clean getaway.*

His master plan was going flawlessly until the shaft did a nine-foot vertical drop, causing him to lose his grip. Charlie shot down the duct at a high rate of speed. The experience must have seemed like a ride at the fair— but the ride came to a sudden and painful stop.

Charlie's air shaft ended approximately three feet above a cross beam that separated two offices. And Charlie reached terminal velocity at about the same time he reached the cross beam. With a force hard enough to break through two ceilings (one leg on each side of the beam), he came to a crushing halt.

Charlie's legs were now in separate rooms. His arms were wedged tightly inside the shaft, straight up over his head. He was snugly straddling a cross beam.

Charlie spent a long weekend waiting for help. It arrived two days later, in the form of the police responding to a "breaking and entering" call. But then the police had to wait for the fire department to come and extricate Charlie from his predicament. As the luckless burglar was led hobbling away, Officer Pete Bell noticed that "part of his anatomy had swollen up to grapefruit size. And being from Florida, we know our grapefruits."

Beavers was arrested and charged with breaking and entering. Most officers on the scene agreed that Charlie had served his sentence long before the police ever arrived.

Oh, did we mention that it rained all weekend, right down the shaft and onto Charlie's face?

Sticky Situation

49

Metropolitan Nashville Police Officer Jeb Johnson gave *America's Dumbest Criminals* this scoop about an alarming crime:

While browsing at a chic clothier, nineteen-year-old Jonathan Parker decided that he needed three leather jackets in the worst way. The price was a little too steep, though, so Jonathan decided that he would take a "five-finger discount." That is, he was going to steal them.

Jonathan surveyed the premises and spotted every shoplifter's nightmare, a sensor alarm in front of the shop's exit. He knew the merchandise was tagged with magnetic strips, and if he tried to slip out with any tagged merchandise, the sensor would set off a deafening siren.

Undaunted, Jonathan grabbed some jackets that suited his taste and ducked into the nearest dressing room. Thoroughly searching the jackets, our shoplifter found all the magnetic strips and peeled them off. He found them inside sleeves and pockets, under collars and along the waistband. Jonathan was very proud of himself as he flicked the last of the strips onto the floor. He stuffed the jackets under his coat and boldly walked toward the front door.

A second later the loud, piercing scream of the alarm alerted the security guard, who quickly apprehended our thorough young thief. Jonathan was stunned. Hadn't he searched every inch of those jackets?

The security guard searched the stolen jackets, and he couldn't find any magnetic strips either. So why had the alarm gone off?

Then the guard looked a little deeper. He looked right into the sole—the sole of Jonathan's shoe, that is. And there he discovered four or five of the little magnetic strips, which Jonathan had thrown to the floor and then stepped on. The young man was arrested and charged with shoplifting.

Sticky fingers and sticky shoes—they'll get you every time.

Big Brother Is Watching You

Officer Pete Peterson, now an instructor at the Federal Law Enforcement Training Center in Brunswick, Georgia, was working patrol in a much burglarized Illinois neighborhood several years ago. There had been a robbery in the neighborhood and the perpetrator had been arrested, but the police were looking for a possible pickup car. Officer Peterson stopped a vehicle that fit the profile that had been circulated. He asked the driver for his license, and the man quickly complied.

Peterson glanced at the license, did a quiet double-take, then asked the driver to repeat the information on the license. The driver again cooperated. After several minutes of questioning, however, Peterson said, "I don't think you're Mark Peterson."

"What?" the driver protested. "No, that's me!"

"I don't think so," Peterson repeated.

"I don't know what you're getting at," the driver retorted

indignantly. "But I can't stand here all day. I've got an appointment."

For several more minutes he kept insisting the driver's license was his and that Pete was wasting his time.

Finally, Officer Peterson showed him his name badge. "You see, my name's Peterson. I've got a little brother named Mark, and this is his driver's license. My folks live at the address listed here. So I'm pretty sure that you stole this license!"

The driver just sank. "This has been the worst day for me," he sighed.

The day got even worse when he heard the jail door slam shut. He had three outstanding felony warrants for his arrest.

How well do you know the dumb criminal mind?

You're in Raritan, New Jersey, and you've just received a ticket. Now, let's play the matching game. Match the offense with the penalty.

OFFENSE	FINE
a) Littering	$500.00
b) D.U.I.	$250.00
c) Cursing in Public	$25.00
d) Public Display of Affection	Not an Offense

Answers: (a) $25.00 (b) $250.00 (c) $500.00 (d) usually not an offense—depending, we suppose, on how affectionate you get!

Going My Way?

It seems that some people go out of their way to get into trouble. That's more or less what happened the night that Nashville Police Officer Floyd A. Hyde unexpectedly became involved in a high-speed chase.

"I was en route to a personal-injury accident in West Nashville, and to get there I had to enter Interstate 40 from I-440. As I merged, blue lights and sirens going, I fell in behind a gold Pontiac Firebird that suddenly seemed to sprout wings and take off down the interstate. The driver apparently panicked at the sight of me. He accelerated to more than a hundred miles per hour and began passing cars on the shoulder. It was obvious that he thought I was after him and was making a run for it."

But Hyde couldn't give chase, despite the driver's reckless behavior. Injured people always take priority over traffic offenders, so the officer had to stay en route to the accident. But he did try to keep the Firebird in sight as he drove, hoping another nearby unit would be able to

"I saw fire billowing out from underneath that car, with blue smoke and oil going everywhere. He'd blown his engine. Now he had to stop."

step in and stop the speeding vehicle. As it turned out, keeping the Pontiac in sight was not that difficult. Every turn the Pontiac made was the very turn the officer needed to get to the accident scene.

Hyde followed the Pontiac all the way to his destination. At that point he found another unit had already arrived at the accident scene. His help wasn't needed. Now he was free to try to stop the nut in the Firebird, who by this time had developed something new to panic about.

"Just about the time my priorities changed," Hyde says, "I saw fire billowing out from underneath that car, with blue smoke and oil going everywhere. He'd blown his engine. Now he had to stop.

"After I arrested him, I asked him why he was running. He told me he had a suspended driver's license. When I told him that I hadn't been after him in the first place, that I would have simply gone around him if he hadn't taken off like that, *and* that I wouldn't have caught him if he hadn't made every turn I needed to make—well, he got pretty upset."

That incident cost the driver of the Firebird plenty—a thousand dollars for the new engine plus the expense of having his car towed—not to mention the charges for driving with a suspended license, attempting to elude, and reckless driving.

Asleep at the Wheel

Officer Lynn Flanders of the Escambia County Sheriff's Department in Pensacola, Florida, was dispatched to a convenience store where a man was exposing himself. Another female officer quickly joined her as backup. They arrived to find the flasher still on the scene—but sound asleep!

"The flasher was seated in his car in front of the store, totally naked, and snoring up a storm. So we knocked on the window and woke him up."

Flanders then explained to the snoozing streaker that he was under arrest for indecent exposure.

The sleepy-eyed criminal didn't seem all that perturbed, but he did have one request of his arresting officers: "Can I put my clothes on?"

The officers glanced around the car. The only clothes visible in the car were a pair of scuffed shoes and a wad of dirty socks lying on the passenger-side floorboard.

"Well, sir," Flanders told him, "you can put your shoes on if you want to, but I honestly don't think it'll make much difference!"

"Oh, no, Officer," the naked man explained earnestly. "My clothes are here. They're just stuck between the seats here."

Of course. Isn't that where we all keep our clothes when we sleep naked at the roadside convenience store?

Always willing to serve the public, the two officers helped the suspect retrieve his clothes and waited for him to dress before escorting the fully clothed and wide-awake flasher to his new temporary home in a holding cell.

I Can't Believe It

Once when Officer Donna McCown was working narcotics in a large southwestern city, her department head assigned her to secure two hundred dollars' worth of crack cocaine from a known drug dealer who had been arrested several times.

McCown had some concerns about the assignment because, as she remembers it, "I'd been around him before and he should have known who I was." Not only had she been present in the station when he was being booked; she'd also driven around his neighborhood in a marked car and full uniform. She was afraid he might recognize her. But she didn't realize just how dumb this guy was.

"We met in a motel room that had already been wired for the meeting," McCown says. "About ten officers were waiting for me outside. The gentleman showed up as expected, but he seemed a little leery at first. He questioned me as to whether I was a police officer, and I responded that I was not, so we proceeded to do the deal."

But the dealer's jumpiness continued, increasing Mc-Cown's concerns. Had he recognized her? Was he laying some sort of trap, waiting for her to give herself away?

"This looks like good crack," she said as loudly as she dared. This was the signal to her backup that the dealer had sold her the dope. But had she said it too loud? Something was clearly wrong, because the dealer grew more fidgety than ever. "Yeah, sure," he muttered, his eyes darting around the room as he stowed away his two hundred dollars. "Listen, I gotta go now. Got an appointment on the other side of town."

It turned out she needn't have worried about the dealer recognizing her. He had other things on his mind.

Tests revealed there was hardly any crack in the concoction he sold her. It had been cut with all sorts of weird stuff, but mostly a sugar substitute. It wasn't real cocaine. It wasn't even real sugar. The man had been so embarrassed about the quality of his product and so worried that she would realize how bad it was that he had barely glanced at her.

"I can't believe you did that to me," the dealer blurted when McCown and her colleagues arrested him and confiscated his car—rather, his girlfriend's car.

"I can't believe you didn't know me!" she retorted. "And I can't believe you're selling Equal for $850 an ounce. It's a lot cheaper at the grocery store!"

Hop in Back

Officer Lynn Flanders, our Florida friend, had a strange experience with a drunk driver one evening.

"I was pulling over a speeder one night when he put the car in park and jumped into the backseat," she said. "I didn't know if he was going for a weapon or not, so I called for backup.

"In the minute or two that I waited for backup, the couple in the car seemed to be having a fight. They were arguing so loudly I could hear them from my squad car."

When Flanders's backup arrived after a few minutes, she cautiously approached the car she had stopped and peered in the window. A woman sat in the passenger seat with her arms crossed and a furious look on her face.

Flanders asked the woman what she was doing.

"I don't know, Officer," she responded. "Why don't you ask the rocket scientist in the back?"

She gestured toward the disheveled-looking man in the backseat, who looked back with bloodshot eyes.

"Hey, I don't know what's going on," he said with slightly slurred speech and an air of aggrieved innocence. "I've been asleep back here the whole time. Just woke up a minute ago."

"He didn't say that the woman had been driving," Flanders recalls. "If he had, I believe she would have been much harder on him than the courts. So he just went with the ghost-driver theory.

"We ran a check and found out he had several warrants on him. He was arrested for D.U.I."

And poof! Suddenly, he disappeared into the criminal justice system.

Good Thinking

55

To police officers accustomed to hearing outrageous lies and absurd alibis, a truly honest answer can feel like a breath of fresh air—even if that breath has a distinct smell of alcohol. Captain Don Parker of Pensacola, Florida, received such an answer late one night when he stopped a woman he suspected of driving under the influence.

"By the time I got out of my patrol car," Parker says, "she was already out of her car, staggering back and forth, and obviously very upset with me."

"Why are you stopping me, Officer?" the obviously intoxicated woman drawled before Parker could say a word.

"Well, ma'am, you were weaving all over the road," Parker explained. "And you didn't have your headlights on."

"Oh, I can explain," she replied smartly. "You see, I've been drinking all night, and I'm very drunk."

Parker merely nodded.

"Considering my condition," she finished with unerring and incriminating logic, "I think I'm doing very well."

He had to agree, even as he took her in.

"Oh, I can explain. You see, I've been drinking all night, and I'm very drunk. . . . Considering my condition, I think I'm doing very well."

 # Read My List

Her second day on the job, a rookie undercover officer in Florida was assigned to purchase some prescription drugs from a known pill dealer. She was given a list of pills to buy and the quantity needed for a good "bust."

"I wasn't familiar with any of them at the time," she remembers. "I had to write down the names of all the drugs and take the list with me."

When the officer arrived at the "Pill Palace" with her shopping list, she began placing her order. "You'd think the dealer might have been a little suspicious since I couldn't tell her what I wanted without consulting my list. I was awful . . . I kept mispronouncing the drugs' names, and she would even correct me."

The suspect sold the officer $250 worth of stolen pills and was arrested moments later.

"I saw her later at the station and heard her asking if anyone had an aspirin. Ironic, isn't it? She had every pill you could imagine, but didn't have an aspirin!"

If You Can't Beat 'Em . . .

Several years ago in Arkansas, a man robbed a pharmacy clerk at knife point. A few days later, the clerk picked the man out of a photo lineup and pressed charges against him. When the case went to trial, however, the man was nowhere to be found. He had fled the state, and officials had no clue where. They knew he came from New York City, but couldn't be sure that was where he had gone, and they didn't know where in New York to look. They really didn't have much hope of catching him.

Then they got the break they needed to find their criminal. Sure enough, the suspect had returned to New York and had applied for a job. Federal authorities were alerted when the man's prints were sent to Washington, D.C., as part of a standard check required for that particular job application. The man was soon arrested, charged, and convicted.

Oh, and he didn't get the job he applied for—that of police officer.

58 Camera Hog

An officer in Indiana told us of a very photogenic crook who insisted on arranging his own close-ups. This criminal specialized in safecracking. He was highly skilled, extremely thorough, and—at the same time—incredibly dumb.

Our safecracking star had targeted a small local business that kept more than seven thousand dollars in cash in a safe. There were no alarms, and the safe was an older model, relatively easy to crack. But when the criminal arrived at "work," he discovered a couple of video surveillance cameras in the building.

That wouldn't do. After all, nobody likes to work with someone watching over his shoulder, right? So our resourceful crook set about making his workplace more comfortable. He found a ladder, climbed up with his screwdriver, and proceeded to take the lens off each camera.

Now, the big problem with most video surveillance is that you really can't get close enough for a really good picture of the criminal's face. The quality is not that good, and the perpetrators are usually too far away for the ceiling-mounted cameras to capture a good image. But our star safecracker took care of that problem for the local police. While he diligently worked with his screwdriver right in front of the camera, he also provided the officers with the best close-up they'd ever seen—right down to the smallest wrinkle and mole. Meanwhile, the camera across the room was providing a full-length view of him working on the first camera.

The video was picture-perfect, and the safecracker was quickly apprehended.

Smile—you're a dumb criminal!

# **Another Crime of Passion**

It's an age-old story of love, lust, and automobiles—with a new twist brought on by the current Age of Litigation.

A young couple became amorous in a car parked along their town's notorious Lover's Lane. They were in the throes of passion when another car pulled in slowly in front of them. The driver considerately turned off his lights. But then, trying to back up in the dark, the new arrival bumped into the lovers' car.

The couple sued the other motorist's insurance company for child support. The lovers claimed the fender bender outside the car caused another little accident inside the car. The bump from the untimely collision allegedly caused them both to momentarily "lose control"—and the result was an accidental pregnancy.

That's one for the record books—the first and only case (we hope) of a fender bender resulting in a "love child."

Once Bitten, Twice Bitten

60

Sergeant Doug Baldwin in Pensacola, Florida, was dispatched to assist in a high-speed car chase. He responded immediately and soon was hot on the tail of the speeding vehicle.

Suddenly, the suspect's car veered off to the side of the road. The driver's door sprang open, and the driver bolted from the car. By the time Baldwin could get out of his own car and follow on foot the suspect had disappeared.

A search of the fugitive's car uncovered a quantity of drugs. Now he was wanted for possession, speeding, and resisting arrest. But he was nowhere to be found. An extensive canvass of the area proved fruitless. After hours of searching, the officers were ready to call off the search, but Sergeant Baldwin decided to again check the area.

Looking behind an auto mechanic's shop, Baldwin heard something. It sounded like a man whispering "ouch" and quietly cursing. Officer Baldwin traced the sound to a car up on blocks. He bent down, looked underneath the car, and saw a bare-chested man twitching wildly on the ground.

The officer called to the squirming man, who identified himself as the suspect. "You're under arrest," Baldwin said.

"Okay, but hurry up!" the man pleaded. "You've got to get me away from all these mosquitoes; they're about to bite me to death!"

Sergeant Baldwin dragged the man from under the car and saw that his skin was as bumpy as a rhinoceros's hide from mosquito bites. He handcuffed the suspect and was leading him out of the fenced compound when, from out of nowhere, two security dogs appeared and jumped the bad guy. They bit him several times before Sergeant Baldwin could run them off.

Between the mosquitoes and the dogs, the man had about one hundred bite marks on his body. It was a bad case of "overbite"—and a stellar example of taking a bite out of crime!

All Aboard!

When Nashville police officers Andy Wright and Jeff Cherry observed a possible drug buy in a known high-drug-sales area, they approached the man who had made the buy. But when they began to question him, the criminal struck Officer Cherry in the face and took off running. The chase was on.

For nearly half a mile, the officers pursued the suspect on foot. Then he ran down an embankment and over some railroad tracks into a rail yard, crossing just in front of a long freight train, Cherry said.

Officers Wright and Cherry came to a sudden halt as a train barreled down between the officers and the suspect. Says Cherry, "The train separated us from him, but we knew he couldn't run up the other side because more police were coming from that direction."

The two officers knelt down and watched the unbelievable scene that unfolded.

"Looking under the train, we could see the suspect standing there. We watched him closely because we might lose him if he simply ran next to the train," Cherry said.

Instead, standing perfectly still, this genius reached out and tried to grab the handrail on the train, which was moving at about forty miles per hour. It immediately knocked him to the ground and bounced him about ten feet down the tracks.

"We couldn't believe he did that. It's amazing that his arm wasn't yanked off," Cherry says.

The rocket scientist staggered to his feet and tried to jump on the train again. From a standing start, he just sort of threw his body up against the moving train. It knocked him down once more, only more violently this time. This time he didn't get up. His second attempt to jump the train had left him unconscious.

"We waited another couple of minutes for the train to pass while the suspect just lay there. After the last car went by, we scooped him up and took him to the hospital. They kept him overnight for observation, and he was booked on the following day."

The bad guy now knows the difference between a rail yard and a prison yard. Let's hope he also studies basic physics while he's in the joint.

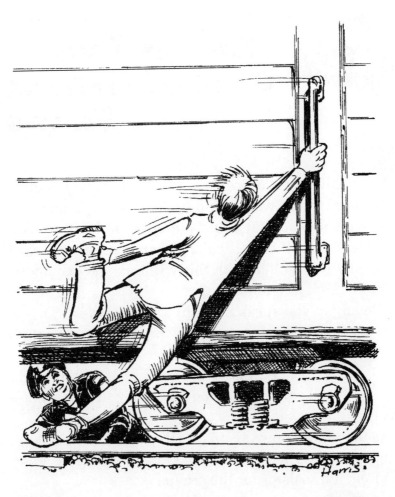

"We couldn't believe he did that. It's amazing that his arm wasn't yanked off."

145

Life Is Like a Pair of Brown Shoes

An immigration officer was sick and tired of dealing with illegal aliens who would pretend not to understand any English for several hours and then suddenly speak it fluently. So on this particular evening when the agent stopped a truck filled with thirty illegals, he decided to try something different.

"Do any of you speak English? *¿Habla Inglés?*"

Every head shook no, and every face looked very quizzically at the frustrated officer.

"Okay, well, look, I'm really tired of this. I'm gonna shoot you all, and I'm going to start with the people wearing brown shoes."

As the officer drew his pistol, three men looked down quickly at their feet. They quickly and gladly accepted the role of translator for the group.

The Clothes Make the Man . . . Dumb!

Dwayne Carver was a maintenance man at the Cedar Wood Apartments in Virginia Beach, Virginia. He had a good job, his own tools, and a blue uniform that read "Cedar Wood" on the back and "Dwayne" on the front.

Now, if you were going to rob a 7-Eleven store, as Dwayne did, you would probably wear a ski mask, as Dwayne did. But you probably wouldn't wear your work uniform . . . yes, as Dwayne did.

When he approached the clerk, his face was completely covered. He even made his voice sound deeper as he ordered, "Give me all the money." The clerk stared at Dwayne and his name tag and handed over several hundred dollars. Dwayne fled to a carefully concealed rental car that he had rented just for the day so that he couldn't be traced.

The police arrived shortly, and the clerk was asked to give a description of the robber. "All I can tell you is that he was wearing a ski mask and a blue maintenance uniform with "Cedar Wood" on the back, and "Dwayne" on the front."

The two officers looked at each other. Surely not . . . no, this was too easy. Maybe the thief stole the uniform or purchased it used at Goodwill. . . .

But it was Dwayne, all right. When the officers appeared at his apartment, he hadn't even changed clothes. The ski mask? It was in his back pocket. The gun? It was in his other back pocket. The money? It was in his front pocket.

You know, this guy's story would have made a great B horror movie back in the fifties. Can't you just picture the title now, slowly dripping down the screen?

Now Showing: The Dwayne with No Brain!

Potted Plants

Back in the fifties and the sixties, drugs weren't as prevalent as they are today. And folks in small towns and rural areas were not "hip" to drugs—or so many city dealers and users thought. A dumb criminal with this attitude ran into trouble one day on the main street of a small Indiana town with a not-so-dumb police officer.

Sitting in his squad car just watching traffic on a warm afternoon, Officer Larry Hawkins (not the same Larry Hawkins mentioned earlier in this book) spotted a Ford station wagon with out-of-state license plates—and a rear compartment full of marijuana plants.

"I guess he just figured our little town has a bunch of backward cops who don't know what marijuana looks like," Hawkins said. "Well, I knew what it looked like. I just took off after him, and he didn't run."

The officer pulled the station wagon over and walked

up to the driver's window. "Partner," he said, "I hope for your sake that those plants are plastic."

The man just looked at the officer with a pleasant look on his face and said, "Yeah, they are."

"Well, I'm sure you won't mind if I just kind of check it out."

For a long moment the driver just looked at the woman in the seat next to him. Finally, he shrugged. "Sure."

So the officer went back and opened the tailgate and pulled out seven live marijuana plants—each one in its own pot. They were full-grown plants—the top of each one bent down by the roof of the car. And they were definitely not plastic.

The smart guy was arrested. The sheriff's office used the plants to show schoolchildren what marijuana looks like. And Hawkins had the last laugh on this city slicker.

"They used to make rope out of hemp, which is marijuana," Hawkins says. "This guy had just enough to hang himself."

Once a
Soldier . . .

Occasionally, we receive a story here at *America's Dumbest Criminals* headquarters that doesn't involve a dumb criminal, but does involve the police and their ability to defuse potentially volatile situations. There's no criminal in this case, just an unfortunate fellow whose straw, so to speak, didn't go all the way to the bottom of his glass—and an experienced cop who handled a delicate situation with creative efficiency.

"Sometimes an officer has to fly by the seat of his pants," says C. R. Meathrell, chief of the Salem City Police Department in Salem, West Virginia. "And being able to ad lib at the drop of a hat can be a real plus."

Several years ago, when Meathrell was a sergeant working the night shift, he was called to a rest home to take care of a disturbance. An elderly patient had refused to take his medication and had mentally reverted to his days as a private in the army. The old soldier had raised enough pure hell that everyone on his floor was awake.

For well over an hour he had paced the hallway, ranting and raving about the expected German attack. The home had called the police to help them with a transfer to a nearby hospital.

"I had a rookie with me who was still trying to find his way around our little town," Meathrell remembers, "and all the way there he was plotting how we would take this guy. I had to remind him that it was just an old man with a bolt or two loose, not a Charles Manson."

When the officers arrived, staff members were waiting to escort them to the old fellow's room. When the rookie and the uniformed sergeant entered the room, the old man stared at the sergeant's rank stripes and then snapped to attention.

"Sergeant," he blared, "I've been a good soldier. Let me show you my medals." With that, he popped open a cigar box with several figurines in it.

Here's my chance, Meathrell thought.

"Private," he barked, "we are here to get you out of enemy territory. But we must hurry; the enemy isn't far behind."

The elderly "private" snapped to attention again, gathered his duffel bag, and marched out the door.

All the way down the hallway, the sergeant called cadence, and the little group marched out the front door as

The elderly "private" snapped to attention again, gathered his duffel bag, and marched out the door.

if they were going to war. Five or six elderly ladies cheered. One elderly gentleman simply muttered, "Nut."

Things went well until the officers and their charge emerged from the door of the rest home. There the good "private" stopped dead in his tracks. He had spotted the fire department ambulance that stood waiting to transfer him. An attendant opened the side door and offered him a hand, but he wasn't having any part of it.

"It's okay, private," the sergeant assured him. "That's a tank I ordered to get you safely across enemy lines. I'll stay behind and guard our flank."

Like a shot, the good old soldier was up and in the ambulance. Meathrell closed the door and waved good-bye.

As the ambulance drove away, the rookie turned to the sergeant with a slack jaw. "A tank?" he asked in disbelief.

"Don't gripe," the sergeant said. "He's on his way, isn't he?"

A Shining Example

66

To some people, image is everything. There are those who would not dream of leaving the house (even someone else's house) without making sure their appearance was in order. And different people have different priorities when it comes to appearance. Some people can't relax unless their hair is neatly combed. Others want to be sure their clothes are in style. For Cecil Warren, shiny shoes were everything.

Cecil was well known on the streets of Roanoke, Virginia, as a small-time thief and occasional burglar. He was just as well known for constantly shining his shoes. It wasn't uncommon for him to put on the spit and polish several times a day. In the end, his particular form of vanity proved to be his downfall.

Cecil had decided to burglarize a house, and he had no trouble getting in. He simply climbed up and over the back porch. Unfortunately, this feat also required him to scramble onto the roof. And roof climbing, as one prosecutor later put it, creates "a great probability of shoe damage." Our vain criminal couldn't get on with the job until he made some repairs.

Cecil escaped from the home with some five thousand dollars' worth of jewelry, but he left behind his can of shoe polish and, more importantly, his *monogrammed* shoeshine rag.

"The can of polish and that rag with the initials C. W. on it were as good as a set of fingerprints," one detective noted.

The vain Mr. Warren was found guilty of breaking and entering and grand larceny. He is now cooling his heels—and probably shining his shoes—in jail.

Always Wear Your Seat Belt

Like any safety-conscious motorist, West Texan Dwight Ketchum put on his seat belt before driving off. Nothing wrong with that, except for the fact that the car he was driving away wasn't his. When the police spotted him, Dwight took flight. The police gave chase.

After a few minutes of weaving through traffic at high speeds and still not being able to shake the police, Ketchum decided to bail out from the stolen vehicle. Pulling over, he flung open the car door and attempted to get out and run. But try as he might, he couldn't free himself from the seat belt.

The police were closing in on him fast. Too fast. Our car thief was apprehended while he was still struggling to get out of the stubborn seat belt.

 # Auto Suggestion

When police officers in a Louisiana city arrived at a vehicle accident call involving property damage, the driver was still on the scene, but not exactly "with it."

In a state of heavy inebriation, Montel Stenson told police that he had simply lost control of his European luxury car. During this momentary lapse, it seemed, he had wiped out an entire fence and slammed into a pole.

Officers on the scene were proceeding through their usual drunk-driver routines when Stenson suddenly went berserk. Running back to his automobile, he started it and began ramming one of the squad cars. Backing up and then hurtling forward, he continued to bash the police vehicle. He succeeded in pushing it up against a nearby garage before police were able to extract him.

What was the reason for this bizarre attack? Stenson told police that his European-made automobile had told him to kill the American-made car.

"I was just following orders," was Montel's truly dumb defense.

You've Come a Short Way, Baby

With all the justified focus on violence against women today, inevitably, there had to be a twist, and *America's Dumbest Criminals* found one in Milwaukee. Hardworking thirty-four-year-old Bjorn Svenson had a tough day on the job. His back hurt, his head hurt, and his exhausted legs felt like wet spaghetti. So he expected sympathy when he told his wife that he was just too tired to attend a rally with her later that evening. Being the long-suffering male martyr that he was, he insisted she go on by herself. "Just don't worry about me."

And that's when she hit him.

"She must've hit me twenty times before I finally blacked out," Svenson said later, after regaining consciousness. "I had just finished telling her that I wasn't going and sat down to take my shoes off. That's when she came up behind me, throwing lefts and rights."

He probably wishes that he had gone to the rally with his wife that night. Badly battered Bjorn suffered multiple injuries from the salvo of fists that rained on him during the surprise assault—a broken nose, a fractured skull, a fractured cheekbone, damage to his cornea, and severe cuts and bruises.

The subject of the rally that night was the problem of domestic violence.

DUMB CRIMINAL QUIZ NO. 367

How well do you know the dumb criminal mind?

While robbing a gas station, the attendant asked the robber for a favor, and the robber complied. Did the attendant ask him . . .

- (a) to hem his pants?
- (b) to let him make one phone call?
- (c) to play the guitar accompaniment for "Dueling Banjos"?
- (d) not to rob the store?

If you answered (b), then you know the criminal mind. The attendant at the Reno, Nevada, gas station was nothing if not bold. "Remember," he told the man who was holding him up, "every victim is allowed one phone call." The robber agreed, and the attendant called the police. Before you could say "reach out and touch someone," the Reno police were asking that dim-witted robber to do *them* a favor: "Would you put your hands in these cuffs, please?"

Don't Pull That One on Me

Although excuses for speeding are more numerous than pocket protectors at a slide-rule competition, this excuse just didn't add up. When an officer clocked a woman driving in excess of twenty miles per hour over the speed limit, he pulled her over.

He leaned into the driver's side window and observed the female driver of the car clutching painfully at her jaw. She mumbled to the officer. "I'b just cum from da dntest an wud goink homb ta git ma med-cine."

After about ten minutes of painfully slow translation, the officer finally deduced that the woman was speeding because she needed pain medication after a long session with her dentist. For some reason, the officer just wasn't buying her story.

"Maybe I better run a check on your license," the officer said, setting his bait. "I seem to remember a woman with this name who was wanted in an armed robbery."

The woman's eyes grew huge and indignant, and her

mouth flew open. "Why, I have never been so insulted in all my life. How dare you accuse me of being a common—"

Then her hand flew to her mouth as she realized she had spoken very quickly and very articulately . . . and that the officer was not likely to overlook her very rapid emergence from the effects of the Novocain.

She was right.

The officer gave her a "tibket"!

Left Holding the Bag

One balmy Florida evening, Officer Joe Briggs noticed a car weaving down the road. The radio was blaring and the heavy bass vibrated the windows in Joe's cruiser. When the driver of the sound machine crossed the double, solid, yellow center line, Joe had seen enough. He popped on his lights and pulled the vehicle over.

The driver failed every field sobriety test in a laughable manner. He was arrested on a D.U.I. charge. His female passenger, however, was released and free to go. The arresting officer called dispatch to phone a friend of the passenger to come get her. But while he was calling he noticed that she bent down, retrieved a small plastic bag from the hem of her pants, and quickly stuffed it down her blouse.

The officer now needed a female officer to search the suspicious passenger. But while he was making that call, the passenger made a run for it. The officer tackled her before she got too far, clapped her in handcuffs . . . and noticed the several other plastic bags of marijuana that had fallen out of her pocket while she ran.

She was arrested for possession of an illegal substance because she had more than one ounce of marijuana . . . and less than an ounce, apparently, of smarts.

72 The Wrong Guy

A man who had been involved in a hit-and-run . . . ran. He knew he was drunk, and he also knew that getting caught would mean a second conviction of driving under the influence. So he got out of his vehicle, stumbled to the next intersection, and flagged down a car at the stoplight.

"I've been in an 'accidentally,'" he drunkenly explained to the driver. "I need somebody to drive me home."

The driver of the car looked at him thoughtfully. "All right," he finally said. "Get in."

The intoxicated hitchhiker couldn't believe his luck. How often do you find such a willing accomplice on the first try? After just a few fumbles he got the car door open and climbed in beside his Good Samaritan.

But then the drunk man noticed something was wrong. True, his head was spinning. But he could swear that the driver had immediately made a U-turn and headed back in the direction of the accident.

"Hey, man, what are you doing?" he asked weakly.

The undercover cop reached under the seat and pulled out his identification and badge.

"Buddy," he said, "this just isn't your day."

73 When You Gotta Go

Captain Pete Bell of the Pensacola (Florida) Police Department was patrolling a nice suburban area when a speeding car ran a stoplight right in front of him. Captain Bell gave chase.

When he had the car pulled over, he approached the driver's side and prepared to write out the ticket. "Sir, I'm going to have to give you a citation for running a red light and speeding."

"Yeah, I know," the man said. "But I've gotta go! I've gotta go!"

Bell was a little taken aback at this guy's apparent lack of concern, even if he was in a hurry to get somewhere.

"Well," Bell said, "you're going to have to wait until I write this ticket."

"I know," the man exclaimed, "but I've gotta go—I've gotta go!"

"Sir, what's your hurry?" the officer questioned.

"Oh, I've gotta go!" came the groaned reply.

"I know you've gotta go—but where?" asked Bell.

"I've *really* gotta go," the man screamed, one arm involuntarily clutching his abdomen. "I have diarrhea. I don't think I can hold it any longer."

Suddenly realizing the situation, Bell quickly tore off the ticket and handed it to the man.

"Here, sir. There's a restroom right across the street at that service station. Have a nice day."

Well, at least now the guy had something to read while he was in the bathroom.

Go Figure . . .

An officer in Florida told us about a dumb criminal who showed up too late to be caught in a "sting"—but still managed to work his way into jail:

"The sheriff's department had set up a fake pawnshop that bought stolen goods. We videotaped all our transactions for several months, then shut the whole operation down and arrested thirty or forty people who had sold things to us. That sting attracted national attention, and the press was having a feeding frenzy—almost nonstop coverage—because the audio and video were so good. We recovered everything from sets of silverware to an eighteen-wheeler."

About a week after the pawnshop sting had been closed, sheriff's department personnel went in to unload their equipment and dismantle the operation.

"We arrived in an unmarked cruiser car that, of course, clearly looked like a police car, with antennas and all. We used a huge truck from the jail with the jail's name

Then the bearded man reached into his pocket and pulled out three stolen Social Security checks. "I'll sell these to you for ten cents on the dollar."

171

printed on the side, two guards, a couple of prison trustees to do the hard labor, and a couple of plainclothes deputies."

They pulled up to the "pawnshop" to find a bearded man sitting on the front steps. He looked at the entourage, recognized one of the undercover agents who had worked the operation, and signaled him to come over.

The agent strolled over to the guy and asked, "What's up?"

"Where've you been?" the bearded man asked.

"We've been around. Why?"

Then the bearded man reached into his pocket and pulled out three stolen Social Security checks. "I'll sell these to you for ten cents on the dollar."

Needless to say, they soon had that man in handcuffs. But as they were putting him in the squad car, the officer couldn't resist asking him a question.

"Didn't you recognize the police units and the security guards and the truck with 'County Jail' on the side?"

"Well, yeah," the dumb criminal answered. "But I just figured you'd stolen the truck and were bringing it down here to sell."

Stop That Thief and Step on It!

A nervous crook sat at an Illinois tavern knocking back beers to "get up his nerve." The beer only managed to shut down his brain while the crook's body went out to rob a nice home. Totally anesthetized, our crook set about breaking into a beautiful ranch house. He tried to pry open a sliding glass door, but he used too much force and broke the glass, cutting himself in the process. The occupant of the house, an older woman who was a very sound sleeper, didn't hear a thing.

Finally, the dumb criminal managed to let himself into the basement. But then he realized he had dropped his flashlight in the yard and couldn't see a thing. Feeling his way around and bumping his shins with almost every step, he managed to find some laundry to tie around his cuts and then to feel his way up the stairs to the first floor.

By now the poor burglar was tired, bleeding, bruised, and still very drunk. He still wanted to rob the house, but first he needed a minute just to lie down and rest. So he felt his way along the walls of the hallway, slowly opened a door, felt his way in at coffee-table height, and finally located an open area where he could lie down. Unfortunately, he got a little too relaxed and soon succumbed to slumber.

At two in the morning the householder woke up and felt a need to visit the bathroom. She swung her legs around to the floor, felt for her slippers, stood up . . . and stepped right on the face of the burglar, who had chosen the floor beside her bed for his nap. He was so far gone that he didn't even stir.

The old saying, "Let sleeping thieves lie," did cross the lady's mind. On second thought, she called the police and had the bumbling intruder arrested anyway.

The Twenty-Eight Daze of February

76

Paul Marguiles, a Nashville police officer, gave *America's Dumbest Criminals* this story about a man with a short-term memory about long months:

On February 25, 1995, Marguiles and his partner stopped a car with a temporary license plate on it in a known drug-traffic area. In Tennessee a temporary tag, as it is known, is made of paper and carries a handwritten expiration date on it. Upon closer examination, they noticed that the tag had been altered from its original expiration date of 2-17-95.

"It did look quite convincing," Marguiles recalls. "The problem was that he had changed the date from 2-17-95 to 2-37-95. It doesn't take a math major to realize that there are only twenty-eight days in February, not thirty-seven."

A search of the vehicle yielded some crack cocaine and a small pipe used to smoke the drug. The car was confiscated, and the driver was arrested for simple possession of a controlled substance, alteration of an auto tag (which is a felony), and driving with a suspended license.

The driver was especially upset when he realized the crack was in the car.

"The car was pretty messy," Marguiles says, "and he apparently didn't realize the stuff was even there."

The only reason he had taken the car out in the first place, he told officers, was that he really needed to buy some drugs.

Name-Brand Robbery

A woman who walked into a Mid-Am Bank in Bowling Green, Ohio, and demanded money from the three tellers inside didn't seem like much of a threat at first. She didn't brandish a gun or threaten anyone with violence, according to Bowling Green Police Chief Galen Ash. (There were no customers in the bank, just the tellers and one bank officer.) She was just an average-looking middle-aged woman, with nothing really desperate or criminal about her appearance or demeanor.

But then, suddenly, the stakes went up. The woman repeated her demand for money and brandished a small hand-held device. She claimed it was a radio remote control that at the touch of a button would detonate a car bomb outside, leveling the bank and killing them all. The bank employees glanced nervously at one another. It was not a threat to be taken lightly . . . or so it seemed.

Suddenly, one of the tellers grew surprisingly and defiantly bold. "I'm not giving you anything," she said as she walked out from behind the counter to confront the would-be bank robber. This courageous teller was quickly joined by her two associates, who jumped the woman, wrestled her to the ground, and held her there until the police arrived.

What made the tellers think that the woman wouldn't detonate the bomb?

According to Ash, "I think their first clue was when they saw 'Sears' on the end of the garage door opener."

Gone Fishin'

A retired sheriff from a sleepy little town in East Tennessee told us this story of the famous Greenback Bank. Yes, that is really its name, and the bank was famous for it. It was also famous for the apparent ease by which it could be robbed. The bank had been hit so many times that at one point they had considered installing a revolving door. Several sweet older ladies worked there, and they never put up a fight or made a fuss, so the bank was famous among criminals for being "easy pickings."

But although the Greenback Bank was easy to rob, it was not that easy to get away from. You see, the bank stood on the main road, and that road was the only way in or out of town. Those sweet older ladies would give the robber the money, then just watch which way he or she went. The police would have a roadblock up and the money back in the bank before the frustrated robbers could think of three ways to spend it.

Well, knowing this, a local fishing guide decided he would try a new approach. He would rob the Greenback Bank on foot, and by the time the police arrived he'd be long gone.

So he did. And he was. The fisherman-robber actually got away clean.

Now, knowing the area like he did, he believed that he had found the perfect hiding place for his loot. He stashed the money in the hollow of an old tree that had grown for years by the riverbank.

He decided to wait until spring before retrieving the stolen loot so that no one would suspect when he "came into some cash." Snug in his cabin, he watched the snow and ice come and then melt away, completely unaware that his money was gradually being withdrawn from the "creek bank." All that thawing had caused the river to rise and flood the riverbank. Now the current was gradually washing away all his money.

That spring provided a bonanza for trout fishermen downstream, who were amazed to begin reeling in truly "big ones." The fishing guide's business, on the other hand, quickly slumped. Who needed a guide when everyone in town could tell where to catch twenty, fifty, and hundred-dollar bills?

Before long, the river was filled with would-be trout fishermen who had learned of the unusual way the stream had been stocked. But the authorities eventually found the source of the muddy money and put two and two together. The robber was eventually caught and convicted.

Unlike the money that went downstream, he went up the river.

The Robber with a Lemon

The Greenback Bank has been robbed many times over its eighty-year history, but the staff will never forget one particular robber. He wasn't particularly bright or very violent, but he did have a remarkable car.

The robber came in with a pistol and demanded money. The tellers smiled pleasantly, complied with the robber's demands, watched which way the robber turned, then called up the road to warn the gas station attendant. The gas station attendant saw the car speed by and called ahead to the police department, who promptly arrested the suspect.

Actually, it might not even have mattered which way this robber turned. Although the crook was surprised at how quickly he was apprehended, no one else was.

As the officer said, "It's not every day you see a 1961 Red Edsel that screams *Arrest me!*"

There were only two cars like it in the entire state.

A Con a Sewer

Gary Michaels of Chicago liked the finer things in life: fast cars, fine art, and expensive jewelry—stuff he couldn't begin to afford. But while peering through the window of the jewelry store, he reckoned his luck was about to change. This was the heist that would get him out of the hole.

Simple: Smash the window, grab the jewelry, and run. Quickly, Michaels spotted a street manhole cover. He pried out the one-hundred-pound disk, hauled it to the window, and heaved it through. Michaels grabbed all the rings, watches, and diamonds he could carry, then took off running. Turning the corner, he almost bowled over a couple doing some late-night window shopping. Panicked, he bolted back into the street, heading for an alley, and then disappeared from sight ... down the open manhole.

The Case of the Beer-Box Bandit

Most crooks who set out to rob a convenience store plan on some sort of disguise, such as a ski mask or even a nylon stocking, to hide their faces and avoid being recognized. But one bandit in East Tennessee wore none of the above. He created his disguise right there on the spot.

Retired officer David Hunter of the Knox County Sheriff's Department remarks that this criminal "had a plan, but his plan just wasn't too deep. He had forgotten to bring along a mask." But then he saw it—an empty cardboard beer box!

The robber entered the convenience store with gun in hand and the beer box over his head. He could just barely see out of the corner of it when he turned the empty case at an angle.

After smacking his knee on the door and knocking over several displays, the man finally managed to face the clerk and demand all the money. She put the money in his hand, and he stumbled and crashed his way out the door.

The robber entered the convenience store with gun in hand and the beer box over his head. He could just barely see out of the corner of it when he turned the empty case at an angle.

The man ran out and hurried to his getaway car, driven by his girlfriend. But she, too, seemed to have difficulty thinking clearly under pressure. When the bandit told her to turn right and head out of town, she turned left and was met by about fifteen sheriff's deputies. She almost literally ran into them. Although it was ten o'clock at night, she had neglected to turn on her headlights.

The clueless couple was captured, then released on bail. And about a week later the aspiring criminal hit on another brilliant plan: He would hit the very same market with the same disguise. The police would never expect it and this time, he'd do it right. Then people would remember him—that daring Beer-Box Bandit.

As it happens, the same clerk was working the night the bandit made his second attempt. She recognized him by his box; the door was locked and the sheriff's department was on its way before the bandit could even enter the store.

It's hard to get away with a box on your head . . . and this dumb criminal didn't. His career in crime was over. And yes, we still remember him—that incredible idiot, the Beer-Box Bandit.

Skid Row

When Bob Ferguson, now a retired police officer in Indiana, responded to a burglary call from a gun store, he learned that the thief had stolen thirty rifles, several handguns, and a number of shoulder holsters, then made a clean getaway. There were no witnesses, no surveillance cameras, and virtually no clues. It seemed this case would be chalked up as a loss.

But Ferguson noticed a set of skid marks on the road where someone had obviously peeled out. He followed his instincts and the skid marks. They led him to a corner, where he found another set of skid marks. Farther up the road were another. The marks mysteriously ended in front of an apartment building. Ferguson entered the building, looked around, and headed upstairs.

Outside the door to an upstairs apartment the officer discovered a leather loop that looked exactly like the leather loop on his own shoulder holster. He knocked on the door, and a man in his early twenties answered.

Ferguson poked the leather loop in the suspect's face. "Where did you get this?"

The suspect responded without a blink, "From breaking into the gun store."

Ferguson's quick thinking and the criminal's quick answer led to quick justice—and a whole new meaning to the phrase, "Keep me in the loop."

Back Door Man

83

Detectives Ted McDonald and Adam Watson of the Brunswick (Georgia) Police Department had taken in a suspect for questioning about a recent homicide. But during the entire interrogation, which lasted several hours, McDonald found himself staring at the suspect's primary identifying feature—his hat.

"I couldn't take my eyes off it," the detective remembers. "It was so big and colorful—I'd never seen anything like it. I kept getting visions of Carmen Miranda in drag. Weird. I guess that hat was his trademark or something.

The detectives felt pretty sure the man with the hat knew more than he was telling, and they suspected he was covering up for some of his buddies. But they didn't really have anything to hold him on, so they finally told him he was free to go. They also told him they were going to talk to his girlfriend to verify his alibi for the night of the murder. He had told them she would support everything he'd said.

"That's cool, man," he said. "You mind takin' me with you when you talk to her?"

Needless to say, the answer was no. The officers wanted to talk to her independently.

"Well, then, can I at least get a ride home?" he asked.

The detectives knew the suspect and his girlfriend both lived in the projects, and he didn't have a car. "Sure," they said, "we'll drop you off at your place, but you can't talk to your girlfriend before we do."

After taking the hat man home, the detectives drove six blocks over and began looking for the girlfriend's apartment.

"It took us a few minutes to find her place," McDonald's partner, Adam Watson, says.

As soon as the detectives knocked, they heard a commotion coming from behind the door—bottles being knocked down, furniture being tripped over, hurried footsteps, and then the slamming of the back door. The man's girlfriend answered the door and gave them permission to enter. But before they began to question her, something in the center of the living room caught their eye.

It was the hat—Carmen Miranda's hat, or, rather, the suspect's hat, left on the table in his haste to beat it out the back door. In the course of five minutes the hat man had run six blocks to his girlfriend's, come in through the back door, told her what to say, and then run out again.

Pretty impressive . . . except for the hat part. Now they knew for sure that he'd been there.

His girlfriend, being smarter than he was, didn't want any part of his lies. She wouldn't corroborate anything he said.

"I think she had just about had it with this joker anyway," McDonald says.

The man was rearrested and, as it turned out, knew more about the homicide than he had let on. The case was later solved.

McDonald sums it up: "He might have had a chance with her if he hadn't left that one-of-a-kind hat sitting on the table. Once we saw that, she couldn't have lied to us if she had wanted to.

"It's funny, though. Every time I see an old Carmen Miranda movie . . . I think of that guy."

Step by Step

If we were stupid enough to risk jail or prison by breaking into a business and stealing something, we'd go for something big, and we'd take every precaution to cover our tracks. But we're not that stupid. That's why we're writing a book and a certain man in Wisconsin is writing his wife.

It had snowed off and on for most of the day. There wasn't a lot of moisture in the air, but there was enough to keep the snow from being blown away by the gusty winter wind.

Toward evening, the police received a call on a 2-11, a burglary. When they arrived at Bernie's Barbershop, they saw that the window had been broken out in the front of the small free-standing building. There really wasn't that much in there to steal. It was a modest two-chair shop.

Bernie the barber was called down to the shop to meet with the officers and take a look at the damage.

"Can you tell us what's missing from your shop, sir?" a young uniformed officer asked the man.

"What's the matter with people today?" the barber mused disgustedly. "I'm a working stiff. What's some jerk doing stealing from a working man?

"Sure, I can tell you what's missing, Officer," Bernie steamed. "My brand new portable color television set that I haven't had long enough to even have to dust yet—that's what's missing! I'd just like to know where the bum that took it is right now!"

It didn't take the officers long to find the answer.

While Bernie talked with the officers, one of the detectives on the scene had discovered something. Footprints. Not the footprints of the officers and Bernie; they were all mixed together in front of the store. No, these footprints led away from the others. Around the corner, past the row of dilapidated houses that lined the block, and down the snowy sidewalk.

Pedestrian traffic had been light that evening, so this particular set of prints was easy to follow. They continued across the street and down the opposite sidewalk. The detective followed them. The uniformed cop followed the detective. Bernie followed the officer.

The prints led to an apartment complex, then to a door, and disappeared behind it. The detective rapped sharply on the door. After a short wait, a nervous woman appeared.

"Yes?" her voice quavered. The detective was looking down. A set of wet footprints still covered the carpet and led right to a large sofa where an even larger man sat watching a hockey game on Bernie's TV.

The reception on Bernie's stolen television was perfect. The only snow was on the man's shoes, the only fuzziness was between his ears. And before the game was over, the larcenous hockey fan was looking at a different station . . . the police station's penalty box.

Dressed for Arrest

Sergeant Larry Bruce told *America's Dumbest Criminals* about a routine warrant he served one morning that took an unexpected twist and became a comedy of errors.

There had been a string of burglaries in the city of Brunswick, Georgia, and Bruce had been put on the case.

"I had a pretty good idea who the person was," Bruce says. "In a town of just seventeen thousand people, if you've been around for a while, you get to know what's going on and who's doing it."

When Bruce had collected all the evidence he needed, a warrant was issued for the suspect's arrest. Sergeant Bruce and another officer set out early on a February morning to serve the warrant. They were hoping to save some effort by catching the suspect while he was still in bed.

"It was exceptionally cold that morning—about twenty-eight degrees," Bruce recalls. "My partner and I walked up the crooked sidewalk to the front door of the man's mother's house. 'This shouldn't be too hard,' I remarked to my partner.

"Well, his mother answers the door and tells us that her son is already up and in the bathroom. So we explained that we needed to talk to him, and would she be kind enough to go and get him for us. Which she did. She returned a moment later with her son right behind her. He wore white jockey shorts, and his face was covered with shaving cream.

"As soon as he saw us he 'booked.' We couldn't believe it at first. The guy runs to the back of the house and out the bathroom window—in his underwear at twenty-eight degrees!"

Still shaking their heads, the officers ran to the squad car to radio for help.

"In foot pursuit of a black male . . . six-foot-two . . . about one hundred and ninety pounds . . . wearing white Fruit of the Looms and a face full of shaving cream . . . send all available units."

The dispatcher was incredulous. "We didn't copy all that. Please repeat."

Bruce repeated the bulletin. Midway through, he realized how it must sound and began to laugh. It took a minute or so to repeat the information. By then both officers were laughing.

"In foot pursuit of a black male . . . six-foot-two . . . about one hundred and ninety pounds . . . wearing white Fruit of the Looms and a face full of shaving cream . . . send all available units."

After a few more minutes, several units had arrived in the neighborhood and an intensive search had begun. As the officers combed the neighborhood, people were coming out for their morning papers.

"Y'all looking for a crazy man runnin' around in his underwear?" one old man asked.

"Yes, we are. Have you seen him?"

"Just turned the corner to the left," he responded with a cackle. "Don't worry 'bout him. He was movin' too fast to freeze!"

The officers turned another corner. A woman in a housecoat stood pointing to a vacant house on a corner lot.

The officers converged on the house, and Bruce knocked. The door swung open. There stood the suspect, still in his undies, and still wearing the shaving cream, which by now had dried out a little. He yawned innocently, stretched, and said, "You looking for someone, Officer?"

"Yes, you!"

The man protested that he had just awakened and was shaving when the officer knocked. The fact that there was no furniture, no running water, no electricity in the house didn't really seem to bother him. Neither did the fact that everybody in town knew the house had been empty for more than a year.

The suspect, now shivering, was escorted to the closest squad car. Bruce and his partner headed around the block to their own unit.

"No, Larry," laughed the other officer as he turned up the collar of his jacket against the cold. "That wasn't hard at all."

Four-Wheel Suspicion

Patrolling a strip of fast-food restaurants in Memphis, two officers spotted a known car thief pulling out from a drive-through window in a car they suspected didn't belong to him. At about the same time, the suspect spotted the patrol unit.

He took off. The cops hit their lights and sirens and started the pursuit.

"We are in pursuit . . . possible stolen vehicle . . . southbound on Washington . . . now heading south onto Adams Street."

"This kid was runnin'," remembers Sergeant Keith Haney of the Memphis Police Department. "We'd dealt with him on numerous occasions in the past, but he was still a minor then, and the courts would let him off easy. He knew this, so whenever he'd steal a car, he would always go for broke when he was being chased by the police. He was a real cocky kid, too. But this was the first time we'd ever been after him since he turned eighteen. Now he was an adult—and could be tried as one."

"Suspect just took out part of a fence at Garden and Greenlawn and is now going the wrong way on Lincoln Avenue."

This was one car thief who was determined not to be caught. For a good twenty minutes he sped through stop signs and red lights, down side streets and back alleys. Finally, surrounded by police units, he abandoned the car and attempted to flee on foot. The officers caught him before he had run twenty yards.

The next day, the new adult was taken to Haney's office for questioning.

"You've got the wrong man," the kid stated boldly. Apparently, he had spent the long night in jail strategizing about how he was going to get out of this one.

"Really?" the sergeant responded. He glanced down at the arrest record. "They identified you in a car that didn't belong to you, chased you for seven miles, then arrested you right after you exited the vehicle. Of course it was you."

The thief shook his head back and forth. "There's no way they could have identified me," he said cockily.

"And why is that?" Haney asked.

"I was wearing a baseball cap," he sneered. "And the windows of the car were tinted."

Quick Comeback

Officer Dan Leger, a southern undercover narcotics officer, was always quick with an ad lib. One story Leger told us really showed the importance of the quick comeback in police work. A creative impromptu answer can be an officer's best tool for handling the situation by controlling the conversation.

"I was working undercover, and I was making a buy. You've got to record everything you can for evidence when the buy goes down, and this means you almost always have to be wearing some sort of 'wire' for recording your conversations. Unfortunately, every dealer knows that, too. Hollywood has always shown the undercover cop putting a wire right on the chest area, so for starters you want to be creative in where you put the wire. But you've also got to be prepared to talk your way out if the bad guys happen to find it. You'd be surprised at what they'll believe."

One criminal, for instance, went straight to Leger's wire and confronted him, blowing the officer's cover sky high. In less than a minute, however, Leger had managed to convince the criminal not only that he wasn't a cop, but also that he was one of the baddest and smartest criminals that particular dumb criminal had ever run into.

When the criminal shouted, "This is a wire! You're a cop!" Leger looked at him like he didn't have a lick of sense and then explained the facts of life.

"Of course it's a wire," he said patiently. "My lawyer told me to wear this so I'd have evidence to prove entrapment if I ever made a buy from an undercover officer. You ought to be wearing one, man. If a cop busts us and we go to court, it's our word against the cop's . . . and who do you think a judge is going to believe? But if you've got them on tape you can blow their case right out of the water."

The dumb criminal was stunned by the logic.

"Wow, that's really true, man. Great idea! Where did you get yours?"

"I told him where he could get a wire, and I also gave him some tips on how to wear it. He thanked me warmly for the information, then he went ahead and sold me the dope. I eventually proved my point in court."

The judge and jury did take Leger's word over the dumb criminal's because Leger had the recording from his wire and that was the evidence that convicted him.

As the Crow Pries

A burglar alarm went off at the station, and Lieutenant Dewey Betts of the Memphis Police Department quickly rolled out. The alarm was from a drug rehabilitation center Dewey was familiar with. When he arrived on the scene, it was obvious that the burglar had broken in through a second-floor window. What was not obvious was why the burglar chose the center. It's not exactly the logical place for a dumb criminal to look for drugs or money.

Betts called for backup and waited for the arrival of the second unit. Meanwhile, he stood with his back against the wall, hidden, in case the crook looked out and saw him standing there.

There was a creaking noise and the lieutenant looked to the side. The crook was trying to make his escape headfirst through the first-floor window. Not wanting the suspect to get away, the officer grabbed the crook by the collar and started to pull him through the window to the ground where he could cuff him. But when Betts pulled, the burglar screamed uncontrollably.

Betts was stunned at the man's reaction. He thought then that he might have an out-of-control drug addict on his hands. He couldn't let the man go because the suspect was in the kitchen and there were too many possible weapons lying around. So he kept pulling. Every time Betts pulled, the burglar screamed louder and louder.

When Betts's backup arrived, they tried to pull the man through the window . . . with the same results. With every tug, the man screamed at the top of his lungs.

Finally, two of the officers went inside the center, got behind the man, and pushed him out of the window into Betts's arms. That's when the lieutenant noticed a shiny object tucked into the burglar's pants. It turned out to be a chrome-plated crowbar that the crook had used to break into the center.

Now everything became perfectly clear. When the crook was leaning out the window with the crowbar wedged down the front of his pants, he had created a painful leverage on his privates. Every time someone pulled on him, the crowbar would act like a small, effective lever and apply enormous pressure on the suspect's groin area. Since the source of his agony was also important evidence in his crime, he didn't really want to tell the officers, "Guys, there's a crowbar in my pants. Could you stop pulling on me, please?"

Needless to say, the lieutenant didn't need to pry a confession out of this particular dumb criminal.

Stealing Home!

It was the early 1990s and baseball would never again be played in the old Comiskey Park in Chicago. Cheering crowds believed they had seen the last play at the historic stadium. Not long afterward, however, two dumb but nostalgic baseball fans decided to try one last half-inning on their own.

The two men climbed onto the field at night with the intention of stealing the old home plate for a souvenir. Silently, they crept over the field with their shovels, peering nervously over their shoulders, jumping at the slightest sound, but determined to obtain their prize. What a collectible!

But surely they paused for just a moment to contemplate, to look up at the silent, shadowy stands and hear the cheers once more. They must have gazed down at that old plate, envisioning all the runs that had been scored from that spot, all the great batters who had stood there, all the great pitchers who had hurled the ball toward home.

They paused for just a moment to wonder how they were going to get away with their crime now that two security guards were running toward them on the field.

There was a frantic rundown play between third and home before the two thieves were captured for the unofficial final out at the old Comiskey Park.

The Fall Guy

We've all heard of people who have been in accidents that could have or should have killed them but were so drunk they weren't even injured. Detective Adam Watson of Brunswick, Georgia, tells about one of those people whose amazing good luck managed to outstrip his sheer dumbness.

Watson was dispatched to an exclusive resort estate late one Saturday night to check on what was supposed to be a break-in with the suspect still on the premises. The terrified occupants of the house, an older couple by the name of Thompson, had whispered the story over the phone when they called police.

Around midnight, the Thompsons said, a man had appeared at the front door of their residence and begun pounding crazily, determined to gain entrance. Not surprisingly, they had refused to let him in. After several unsuccessful minutes the man had moved to the back door and continued his pounding. Then, as the Thompsons were phoning the police, they heard the sound of shattering glass and a loud thud that told them their intruder had somehow gained admittance. They didn't try to find out how. They just locked themselves in their bedroom and waited for the police.

"When we arrived," Watson says, "we began an immediate search of the home with weapons drawn. We came around the corner and entered a hallway on the first floor. And there in a crumpled heap lay the intruder—out cold. But it wasn't until much later, when we got him to the hospital and he woke up, that we were able to piece together what really happened."

The burglar, it turned out, wasn't really a burglar. He was a high-powered executive who had been visiting friends at the resort. That night, he had gotten totally wasted in a local bar and then gotten lost. Drunk and unfamiliar with the area, he arrived at the Thompsons' and assumed their home was the condo where his friends were staying. He had beaten frantically on all the doors, seeking admission.

Getting nowhere, he had next decided to scale the side of the house and climb in through a second-story window. First he tried to open it, then finally he smashed it and fell through.

Unfortunately for him, the window he chose was in a room with a cathedral ceiling. There was no second floor to land on. He fell twenty feet and landed in the first-floor hallway.

When the intruder was finally able to talk to police the next day, he told them that all he remembered was knocking on the door. He had no recollection of climbing up the house or falling twenty feet or being arrested—he was just too drunk to remember anything at all.

"We ended up charging the guy with criminal trespassing," the officer states. "There was nothing else we could charge him with. He really wasn't breaking in, and there was no criminal intent."

And amazingly, the only ill effects he seemed to suffer from his twenty-foot fall were a few bruises.

DUMB CRIMINAL QUIZ NO. 457.2

How well do you know the dumb criminal mind?

A dumb crook tried to rob a gas station, but the attendants didn't cooperate. When neither attendant would hand over the money, did the criminal . . .

- (a) start crying and run away?
- (b) challenge the attendants to an arm-wrestling contest for the money?
- (c) threaten to call the police?
- (d) hold his breath until he passed out?

If your answer was (c), then you're getting the idea. A would-be bandit in Oklahoma grew so upset that the gas station attendants refused to give him the money that he threatened to call the police. When the attendants still refused, the man made good on his threat. Needless to say, he was half-gassed himself at the time.

Wrong Side of the Tracks

No officer likes to get a call involving a train accident. They are usually the bloodiest and most disgusting scenes imaginable.

One evening Marshal Larry Hawkins of Little Rock got a call that a pedestrian had been hit by a train. Expecting the worst, Hawkins reported to the scene. He arrived to find a crowd of spectators craning their necks to get a better look. The marshal elbowed his way through the crowd and saw the victim—standing up talking to someone and brushing off the dirt on his pants.

Here's the story Hawkins unraveled: The man and his wife were at Johnson's Tavern, which is right next to the railroad tracks. They both got drunk, and then they got into an argument. He said to her, "The hell with you, I'm walking home." The railroad track went right past his house, so he decided he was going to walk the tracks home.

Meanwhile, a southbound train was on its way. And

But the important thing is that he was lying between the two rails
when the train went over him.

somewhere between the tavern and home, the train and the drunk man managed to meet.

The conductors and the engineers all saw a man go down, and they were sure the train went over him. They assumed he had been killed. But somehow after the train had managed to stop, the dumb, drunk, and incredibly lucky criminal was still alive.

To this day, no one is sure exactly how it happened. The train might have knocked the man down, or he might have passed out on the tracks. But the important thing is that he was lying *between* the two rails when the train went over him.

Said Hawkins, "Now, there's always stuff hanging down under a train, like air hoses and stuff, and those things did clip him and roll him around. He was bruised, scratched, and cut, and his clothes were torn. But he was all right. He was up and walking around—still drunk and scared out of his mind. I took him in for his own protection and arrested him for public intoxication."

My Name's Steve, and I'll Be Your Dealer Today

Giving one more glance around the crowded bar, Agent Johnson (who's still working undercover in the South somewhere and shall therefore remain otherwise nameless) yawned and sighed. He was working undercover narcotics and had wanted to bust a certain known dealer that night. But the dealer had never appeared. Whatever the reason, the whole evening had been a colossal waste of time.

The agent was about to pay his tab and go home when a man slid onto a stool next to him and struck up a conversation. Johnson began to suspect that this man might also have connections to the drug culture.

"Hey, man," he asked his new acquaintance, "you know where I can buy some reefer?"

The man said evenly, "As a matter of fact, I do." After a few more minutes' conversation, Agent Johnson understood that the man was referring to himself.

216

By now Johnson was wondering, *How am I going to find out who this guy is?* He had to have a name in order to serve a warrant. And he had to serve a warrant, because to arrest the man on the spot would jeopardize the entire operation and blow his cover as well.

The new suspect didn't feel comfortable selling drugs in the bar, so they strolled outside into the parking lot. The man led Johnson to his car. The agent was still racking his brain, trying to think of a way to learn the dealer's name.

Then the dealer himself solved the problem.

"Listen, man, it's nothing personal," he said. "But I don't know who you are. I mean, you could be a cop for all I know. So can I see your driver's license?"

With a rush of relief, the agent pulled out a phony driver's license that he used for undercover work. And then he said, "Hey, I don't know who you are either. Can I see *your* driver's license?"

"Sure," the dealer replied.

The agent looked at his license, memorized the information, and made the buy. About a week later, the dealer was treated with a personalized warrant for his arrest signed by his new friend, Johnson.

93 Hooked on Crime

In a Florida town, the first policewoman on the local force was sent undercover to crack down on the prostitution problem. Her particular targets were the "johns," or clients, who are considered as much a part of the problem as the prostitutes themselves. (After all, it's just as illegal to buy it as it is to sell it.)

The police officer was dressed to look like a "working girl," wired for sound, and sent out to walk the streets. It wasn't long before a well-dressed man picked her up.

"Are you a cop?" the man asked her.

"Do I look like a cop?" she responded.

"Well, no, you look too nice to be a cop."

So the conversation continued, and the man eventually told the undercover officer what he had in mind. But that wasn't enough to arrest him for solicitation, however. He also had to offer to pay her.

"What's in it for me?" the officer asked.

"Well, normally," the man said, "I don't pay more than fifty dollars. But as good as you look, I'd pay you a hundred bucks."

The officer leaned down and spoke into her hidden microphone, "Fellows, did you hear that? I knew I could make a whole lot more money doing something besides being a cop."

The man was flabbergasted. "You are a cop!" he yelled.

The female officer looked at him smugly. "Yes, I am."

"Hell!" the man exclaimed. "If you'd have told me you're a cop, I would've offered you two hundred bucks. I've never screwed a cop before."

"You've been screwed by one now," the officer remarked. "You're under arrest."

A Red-Hot Robbery

In St. Louis, Missouri, two men entered a convenience store with the intention of robbing it. They made their intention known to the clerk—but they had no weapons. The clerk told them that if they didn't leave the store he would call the police.

Frightened that their robbery wasn't working out like the ones on television, the two crooks made a run for it. But one of the robber wannabes decided he was going to steal *something*—so he grabbed a hot dog off the rotisserie and quickly shoved the whole thing in his mouth.

A few steps outside the convenience store, the hot-dog thief collapsed—he was choking on the frankfurter. Faced with this beautiful case of poetic justice—it takes a weenie to stop a weenie—the other man did the only honorable thing a dumb criminal can do. He ran like hell, leaving his partner gasping in the parking lot.

He grabbed a hot dog off the rotisserie and quickly shoved the whole thing in his mouth.

The Five-Year Cab Ride

Late one evening, in a small town in Illinois, a taxi was called to a local bar to pick up a man who had imbibed a bit too heavily. The gentleman in question staggered out to the cab, gave his home address, and slouched back into the seat as the taxi pulled away from the curb.

When they arrived at the guy's house, the drunk told the cab driver that he didn't have any money on him, but that he had some in the house. "I'll just run in and be right back out with the money, okay?"

That was fine by the cabby; it happened all the time. But not quite this way.

The man got out of the cab, staggered into his house, and reappeared a few moments later.

"I couldn't find any money," he slurred, "but I found my gun, so you're going to have to give me all *your* money."

Believe it or not, this guy actually robbed the cab driver at gunpoint, took the money, and then lurched back into his house, leaving the cabby still parked outside.

You don't have to be psychic to see where this is going. The stunned and shaken cab driver backed his vehicle up about a block, called his dispatcher, and told them he had just been robbed at gunpoint, and then described exactly where the armed robber was at the very moment.

When the police arrived on the scene, the cabby repeated his story to them. Then he watched as the police approached the house, weapons drawn.

Pete Peterson was an officer on the force at the time. He remembers that the front door was wide open when the officers approached.

"Only the storm door was shut," Pete recalls, "and it wasn't locked."

The officers looked in through the storm door to the lighted living room. There on the coffee table was the .38-caliber handgun. And there on the sofa, passed out cold, was the robber.

The drunk was sentenced to five years in prison for armed robbery. He might as well have told the cabby, "Take me straight to jail."

 # Winner Loses

Winning the lottery is every gambler's dream. So when Donna Lee Sobb hit the California state lottery for one hundred dollars she was thrilled. Not only did she need the money, but her winning ticket also qualified her for the big two-million-dollar jackpot.

Things were looking up for Donna, it seemed. She smiled as she looked at her picture in the local newspaper. She was getting some attention, and people on the street occasionally recognized her. Unfortunately for Sobb, so did the people on the beat—the police beat, that is. A local cop read her story, saw her picture, and recognized her as the woman wanted by authorities on an eight-month-old shoplifting warrant.

Now Sobb *really* needed that hundred dollars she had just won. She ended up applying it toward her bail.

The Civic-Minded Cocaine Cooker

97

It was October 1993 in a Georgia town when Tyrell Church was in the kitchen cooking up his specialty . . . cocaine. He had been doing that for a good thirty years, but he had never seen any that cooked up like this batch. Something was wrong.

"I had never seen powder cocaine that turned red when you cooked it up," Church explained. So, being concerned for his own welfare as well as that of the public at large, Tyrell Church did what any fool would do. He took the suspicious concoction to the Georgia Bureau of Investigation crime lab for analysis.

The lab ran four separate tests. The substance proved to be cocaine after all. And Church was promptly arrested and charged with possession of the same. He opted to serve as his own lawyer in what to him seemed a ridiculous trial.

"Had I known I was going to be arrested," he argued, "I wouldn't have taken it over to the lab."

So why did Church take his cocaine to the lab?

"If kids get hold of something like this," he said, "it might hurt them or poison them. I took it over there to have it tested to see if it had been cut or mixed with any dangerous substances."

The civic-minded cooker went on to say that if something had been wrong with the cocaine, he could have warned the public.

Church insisted that he had often had his cocaine tested in New York, where he once lived.

"What's the sense in having a crime lab," he asked, bewildered, "if a person can't take anything over there?"

He also requested that the substance be retested, a request which the judge denied.

"I'm not a habitual user," the cooker complained in his final statement. "I use cocaine for my arthritis. It's a waste of the taxpayers' time for this kind of case to come to court. The grand jury shouldn't have even bothered."

"I do not think a violation of the cocaine law is a waste of time," the district attorney countered.

The jury couldn't have agreed more. It took just seven minutes for them to return a guilty verdict.

Cold Cash

In Decatur, Illinois, a house had been burglarized by someone familiar with the family—and familiar with where they kept their money. The cash was all in change—rolls of quarters, dimes, and nickels. And kept in the freezer.

During the investigation, one of the detectives was doing the necessary legwork of asking people in the neighborhood if they had seen or heard anything unusual or suspicious the night of the burglary. One person had noticed a car that was parked in the rear of the residence that evening and was able to provide a rather vague description of the vehicle.

Following up on that sparse lead, the investigator stopped by a neighborhood gas station and asked the attendant on duty if he'd seen a car that fit the vague description or seen anyone that might have looked suspicious to him that night.

"Well," the clerk mused, "there was one fella who came in the station that night and paid for his gas in rolled change. I remember because the money was cold, real cold, like it had been in the freezer or something."

Bingo! The detective asked the attendant if he could identify the man if he saw him again.

"Sure, I could," the man stated. "He comes in here about every day or so and buys gas."

The detective handed the clerk his card.

"If that guy comes in here again, I'd like you to get his license plate number."

The very next day the clerk called with the tag number of the vehicle, and the suspect was quickly apprehended."

"Can you believe it?" the detective asks. "I mean, the guy didn't even wait until the money had warmed up before he started spending it—and he only went one block away."

Bloodhound Blues

During the two years that Dan Leger worked undercover down South as a narcotics officer, he had more than his share of dumb criminal encounters. And he was constantly amazed at the "cop folklore" circulated among criminals—the widespread misinformation about the law and police procedure. He tells this story about his all-time favorite dope:

"I was working undercover narcotics, deep cover. I looked like the nastiest of the nasties. I infiltrated the independent bikers and tapped into some large distribution systems. Over the course of a few months I made several buys from a fairly large supplier. We got to be pretty good acquaintances."

One night Leger and the dealer were sitting around talking, and the dealer got going on the subject of how undercover cops work. Leger could hardly keep a straight face as he listened to the man's ignorance.

"I can always spot a cop," he bragged, "the way their eyes move around a room and the questions they ask."

Then he went on to relate an old hippie myth that originated in Berkeley or someplace similar. The gist of it was that years ago a city council somewhere decreed that undercover officers had to identify themselves as police officers if they were asked a direct question three times.

"Sort of defeats the purpose of going undercover, you know?" Leger laughs. "Now, if that were the law everywhere, you wouldn't have any undercover officers, because they would all be dead now. But this guy has heard this story, and he lets me in on the secret: 'This is the trick the cops don't want you to know. If you ask an undercover cop three times if they're a cop and they don't tell you, then it's entrapment, and the case gets thrown out.'

"It's really hard to look impressed when inside you're laughing your ass off, but I nod my head like I'm committing his every word to memory.

"Then he did it. He really pissed me off. He said, 'I can smell a cop a mile away.' I was sitting about two feet away from him at the time."

Leger had to bite his tongue to keep from saying something right then, but he knew he'd have the last laugh in the near future. And sure enough, about three weeks later he took that dealer down with a rock-solid case.

"I relished the moment," Leger remembers. "I whipped out my badge and got right up in his face and said, 'Guess what? I'm the Man, and you are under arrest.' His face got as pale as a cadaver, and then I just couldn't resist rubbing it in.

"I was an inch from his nose.

"How do I smell from here?"

All's Well That Ends

One rainy night at the state penitentiary in Michigan City, Indiana, three hardened convicts escaped through a dark, muddy field. They had been convicted of everything from armed robbery to murder. Now they were armed and dangerous and had nothing to lose.

They crept up on a dark, still house. The garage door was unlocked, and they walked right into the kitchen. Creeping from bedroom to bedroom, they bound and gagged all four members of the family. One of the criminals rifled through all the jewelry boxes while another found the car keys. The third got the man's wallet for the credit cards. Then they were off.

Back at the prison, a random bed check revealed the convicts' escape. Soon, helicopters, dogs, and numerous state, county, and city units began combing the area. Once the family managed to free themselves and call the authorities, the police had a car description and a tag number.

Within moments a state trooper spotted the stolen family station wagon moving at a high rate of speed on the interstate. He gave chase, and the escapees made a run for it, veering across the grassy median in an attempt to lose the trooper.

As the fleeing car bounced up onto the other side of the highway, the driver lost control. The car rolled three times, and the convict in the backseat was thrown clear into the high grass. Unharmed, he lost no time disappearing into a nearby cornfield.

Two miles away at Ollie Hardison's farm, the silent dawn was shattered by the thundering wash of police choppers overhead and the baying of bloodhounds closing in on a scent. Ollie had several hog sheds out behind his barn that were pretty well rusted out and falling down. He thought he had heard something out there just a moment before, but now he couldn't hear anything for all the commotion.

One of the arresting officers, Larry Hawkins (the one from Indiana mentioned earlier, that is), will never forget the scene that followed.

The fleeing convict had cut through the fields off the interstate, running at top speed through corn nine feet high. When he came upon the dilapidated hog sheds, he tried to get into one. It was too small. But when he heard the choppers and dogs, the desperate man dropped to all fours and backed into the stinking hog shed.

Unfortunately for him, as he backed in, he also backed out. It seems the back of the shed was rusted out to form a perfect picture frame for the convict's posterior, which was totally exposed. As the police encircled the shed, the convict's rear was positioned in a most peculiar way for arrest.

"He really thought he was totally hidden. He looked like an ostrich with his head in the sand. He held perfectly still and we just sort of stared at this big rear end sticking out of that shed. We just had to laugh. We didn't know whether to turn the dogs loose on him, read him his rights, or just give him a good swift kick."

Good sense and professionalism prevailed. The officers and Ollie Hardison were the only ones to get a kick out of the situation. And they did—no ifs, ands, or butts.

"We didn't know whether to turn the dogs loose on him, read him his rights, or just give him a good swift kick."

235